SPACE
DICTIONARY
FOR KIDS

SPACE
DICTIONARY
FOR KIDS

THE EVERYTHING GUIDE
FOR KIDS WHO LOVE SPACE

AMY ANDERSON AND
BRIAN ANDERSON, PH.D.

PRUFROCK PRESS INC.

Library of Congress Cataloging-in-Publication Data

Names: Anderson, Amy (Amy Larissa), 1993- | Anderson, Brian, 1962-
Title: Space dictionary for kids : the everything guide for kids who love
  space / by Amy Anderson and Brian Anderson, Ph.D.
Description: Waco, Texas : Prufrock Press, Inc., [2016] | Audience: Age 9-12.
  | Includes index.
Identifiers: LCCN 2016016763 | ISBN 9781618215154 (pbk.)
Subjects: LCSH: Space sciences--Dictionaries, Juvenile. | Outer
  space--Dictionaries, Juvenile. | Outer space--Exploration--Dictionaries,
  Juvenile. | Astronomy--Dictionaries, Juvenile. | Cosmology--Dictionaries,
  Juvenile.
Classification: LCC QB497 .A53 2016 | DDC 520.3--dc23
LC record available at https://lccn.loc.gov/2016016763

Edited by Katy McDowall

Cover and layout design by Raquel Trevino

ISBN-13: 978-1-61821-515-4

Printed in the United States of America.

At the time of this book's publication, all facts and figures cited are the most current available. All telephone numbers, addresses, and website URLs are accurate and active. All publications, organizations, websites, and other resources exist as described in the book, and all have been verified. The author and Prufrock Press Inc. make no warranty or guarantee concerning the information and materials given out by organizations or content found at websites, and we are not responsible for any changes that occur after this book's publication. If you find an error, please contact Prufrock Press Inc.

Prufrock Press Inc.
P.O. Box 8813
Waco, TX 76714-8813
Phone: (800) 998-2208
Fax: (800) 240-0333
http://www.prufrock.com

TABLE OF CONTENTS

INTRODUCTION

If you're anything like us, you're fascinated by space—from stars, galaxies, and nebulas to black holes and supernovas—even the possibility that while we're searching our skies for signs of alien life, someone—or some*thing*—on some alien planet is searching their skies for us. More than any other branch of science, astronomy amazes us with both facts and possibilities. But in any area of science, a solid grasp of the vocabulary is essential for understanding the concepts. What's the difference between a nova and a supernova? And what exactly is a quasar, anyway?

Of course there's a lot more to astronomy than just knowing what the words mean, and *Space Dictionary for Kids* is more than just a list of definitions. In addition to defining the vocabulary of astronomy, this book provides a deeper understanding of the concepts so that the definitions make sense. If we've done our job right, this book will not only answer many of the questions you have about space, it'll also have you asking new questions that you never considered before.

Astronomy is too vast of a subject to take on all at once, so we have broken this dictionary into four sections. Cosmology deals with the origin and evolution of the universe. The section on Stars and Galaxies contains the vocabulary of deep space astronomy—everything outside of our solar system. The largest section of the book defines words that describe the objects in Earth's immediate neighborhood, The Solar System. This is followed by a section on Astrobiology and Exoplanets, which covers two of the hottest topics in astronomy today—the search for alien life in outer space and the study of planets orbiting other stars. Following the dictionary entries are a section on the history of space exploration, which outlines humankind's attempts to reach out into space; a timeline of astronomy through the ages; and a list of some books and websites that you may find useful in developing a deeper understanding and appreciation of astronomy.

It's our universe—love it and learn it—or leave it!

COSMOLOGY

THE BIRTH OF
THE UNIVERSE

To ancient astronomers, the night sky was populated with eternal, unchanging stars, along with five planets that wandered among the stars, and occasional unexplained bright spots or streaks of light. As far as they could tell, the universe had always been that way and always would be. But as the science of astronomy developed, discoveries suggested that the universe has not always been the way it is now. The new finds suggested that the universe had a beginning and would one day come to an end, and that the universe and everything in it is constantly changing.

Astronomers now believe that the entire universe was once a tiny speck—a gigantic amount of matter contained in a region of space so small it would be impossible to measure. About 13.7 billion years ago that speck exploded from within. It expanded outward in every direction and formed the universe we know today. We call that explosion the Big Bang.

If you've ever set off a firecracker, you've seen the evidence it leaves behind. There are scattered pieces of paper from the shredded firecracker and a burn mark on the ground where it went off. Immediately after the explosion there's a lingering odor in the air from the burnt gunpowder. In the same way, the Big Bang left clues behind to tell us that something had happened. We can plot the movements of the stars and galaxies in the universe and see that the universe is expanding. We can compare the compositions of new stars and old stars and see how the universe today has changed from its earliest form. And we can detect energy waves, called *cosmic background radiation*, that are found throughout the universe and indicate that the universe is still cooling down from its early rapid expansion.

Cosmology is the science of piecing together the clues to figure out how the universe began, how it came to be the way it is today, and what ultimate fate awaits the universe. These are some of the terms cosmologists use when studying the universe.

COSMOLOGY

ABSOLUTE ZERO: The coldest possible temperature. At this temperature all molecular motion stops. Absolute zero is -460°F (-273°C), or 0 on the Kelvin temperature scale. Nothing ever reaches absolute zero, but interstellar space gets down to about 2.7 kelvins (-455°F).

ACCELERATING UNIVERSE: The universe is expanding, and the farther you get from Earth the faster it seems to be expanding—objects that are farther away from Earth are moving away from us faster than objects that are closer to us are. This means the universe is an accelerating universe, in which some unknown force is pushing the universe apart more strongly than gravity is pulling everything together. We call that unknown force dark energy.

ANTIMATTER: The universe is made up almost entirely of ordinary matter, in which protons have a positive electrical charge and electrons have a negative charge. Antimatter particles are exactly like ordinary matter except that they have the opposite electrical charge: Anti-protons are negative and anti-electrons (positrons) are positive.

Ordinary Matter
⊕ Protons
⊖ Electron
Antimatter
⊖ Anti-protons
⊕ Anti-electrons
(positrons)

Do not touch! When an antimatter particle collides with its ordinary-matter counterpart, both particles are destroyed and a burst of energy is released.

BIG BANG: A widely accepted theory in astronomy for how the universe began. According to the Big Bang theory, the entire universe was crammed into an infinitesimally small point that suddenly expanded outward like an inflating balloon about 13.7 billion years ago, and continues to expand today. The chaotic mix of energy and tiny subatomic particles coming off of the initial explosion slowly cooled and came together as protons, neutrons, and electrons, which formed the simplest atoms. Gravity pulled the atoms together to form massive clouds in space, and from there the first stars and galaxies were born.

EXPANDING AND COOLING UNIVERSE

COSMIC ABUNDANCE: After the Big Bang, nearly all of the atoms in the universe were hydrogen and helium, but fusion in stars has created many heavier atoms as well. When astronomers talk about the *cosmic abundance of elements*, they're talking about how common one type of atom is compared to the others. For example, for every one million hydrogen atoms in an average star like our sun, there are about 98,000 helium atoms, 360 carbon atoms, 110 nitrogen atoms, and 850 oxygen atoms, along with lesser numbers of other elements.

How old are you? The hydrogen atoms in your body were formed in the Big Bang 13.7 billion years ago, and the rest of the atoms in your body were formed in stars that exploded long before our sun was born 4.6 billion years ago.

COSMIC MICROWAVE BACKGROUND: The universe is filled with low-energy radiation that doesn't seem to have any particular source, and is found everywhere in space. This is called the cosmic microwave background, or CMB. Astronomers believe this is a sign that the universe is still cooling off after the Big Bang. The CMB is sometimes called the *primal glow.*

Changes in intensity across the CMB (pictured here) show a temperature map of the early universe. This image was created from 7 years of probe data and has taught astrophysicists a lot about the evolution of the universe.

COSMIC RAY: Very high speed protons shooting through space. Some cosmic rays come from the sun, but most come from outside of our solar system, most likely from supernovas or active galactic nuclei. Most cosmic rays are deflected by the Earth's magnetic field or are absorbed by the atmosphere.

COSMOLOGICAL PRINCIPLE: The universe looks more or less the same in every direction from Earth. The cosmological principle is the idea that the universe is pretty much the same everywhere, and that the parts of the universe we can't see look a lot like the parts we can see.

COSMOLOGY

COSMOLOGY

COSMOLOGY: The study of the origin of the universe, along with how it came to be the way it is today and what the ultimate fate of the universe might be.

COSMOS: Sometimes cosmos is used as a synonym for *universe*, but more precisely cosmos means the universe when it is viewed as a single well-ordered system.

DARK ENERGY: A powerful and unknown force that is pushing our universe apart. If the Big Bang pushed the universe out in every direction 13.7 billion years ago, then the combined gravity of all of the matter in the universe should be pulling on everything else and slowing the expansion down. But the opposite is true: Everything is speeding up instead. That means some unknown force is acting against gravity to make the universe expand faster and faster. We don't know what that force is, but we call it dark energy.

DARK MATTER: Dark matter is not simply objects in space that are too dim to be seen. Dark matter is a type of matter that we cannot see at all. It does not give off light and it does not absorb light, and it does not block light coming from stars. Dark matter is completely invisible. The only reason we know dark matter is out there is because it has gravity that affects regular matter. We can see the effect of dark matter's gravity, but we cannot see the dark matter itself.

The MACS J0416.1-2403 galaxy cluster with dark matter colored in blue.

Invisible universe! Only about 5% of the universe is made up of regular matter that we can see. The other 95% is made up of dark energy and dark matter.

E=MC²: Einstein's famous equation that says that a very small amount of mass can be converted into a large amount of energy. When stars fuse small atoms together to create a larger atom, a little bit of mass is lost in the process. This little bit of mass is converted to energy that is given off by the star as heat and light.

ELECTROMAGNETIC RADIATION: Another term for light, including other forms of high-energy and low-energy light that our eyes cannot see. The full range of electromagnetic radiation (called the spectrum) includes radio waves, microwaves, infrared light, visible light, ultraviolet light, X-rays, and gamma rays. Objects in space give off all of these types of electromagnetic radiation. Electromagnetic radiation moves at the speed of light and can travel infinite distances.

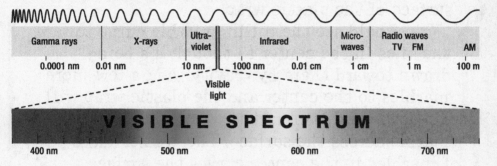

Gamma rays	X-rays	Ultra-violet	Infrared	Micro-waves	Radio waves TV FM	AM
0.0001 nm	0.01 nm	10 nm	1000 nm	0.01 cm	1 cm	1 m	100 m

Visible light

VISIBLE SPECTRUM

400 nm   500 nm   600 nm   700 nm

ELECTRON: A negatively charged elementary particle that orbits the nucleus of an atom. Electrons are very lightweight: 1,836 electrons equal the mass of one proton.

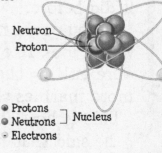

Electron

Neutron
Proton

- Protons
- Neutrons ⎤ Nucleus
- Electrons

ELEMENTARY PARTICLES: Particles that are not made up of smaller particles. These are the basic building blocks that everything in the universe is made from. The most common examples of elementary articles are electrons, quarks, and photons. Protons and neutrons are not elementary particles because they are made up of quarks.

GENERAL RELATIVITY: Albert Einstein's theory that explains gravity: What we see as two objects attracting one another is really due to their masses warping spacetime around them. The theory also says that if you get very close to a massive object like a black hole, time slows down. Experiments and observations in space have supported much of this theory.

COSMOLOGY

Try this!

You'll need a large mixing bowl, some plastic wrap, and some marbles.

Stretch the plastic wrap tightly over the top of the mixing bowl. Use tape or a rubber band to hold it in place if necessary. Set two or three marbles in the center of the plastic wrap. The plastic will stretch lower in the center. Now set another marble near the edge of the bowl and gently flick it across the surface of the plastic wrap.

You should see the rolling marble curve toward the ones in the center as though it's being drawn toward them by gravity. Add a few more marbles to the center and the plastic wrap will dip downward even farther. Try flicking another marble across the surface. The greater mass of marbles in the center curves the surface more, and this time the flicked marble seems drawn even more strongly to the center than it did before.

If you could not see the plastic wrap, it would look like the marbles in the middle were pulling the rolling one toward them, and more marbles were pulling more strongly.

This is how Einstein explained gravity—he said that mass curves the spacetime around it, and objects traveling through spacetime follow the curved surface toward the mass.

GRAVITATIONAL WAVE: In 1916, Albert Einstein theorized that gravity is the result of masses bending the spacetime around them, like a bowling ball placed on a bed curving the surface of the mattress. Einstein also suggested that an accelerating mass would create moving ripples in spacetime. He called these ripples gravitational waves and said that gravitational waves would be able to transfer energy over long distances through space. In 2016, scientists announced that gravitational waves had been detected for the first time.

GRAVITY: A pulling force that causes all objects to be attracted to other objects. The more mass an object has, the stronger its gravitational pull, and the closer you are to the object, the more you will feel its pull. Gravity exists throughout the entire universe, and the same force that causes a dropped pencil to fall to the floor is what holds all of the stars together in the Milky Way.

HELIUM: The second smallest kind of atom in the universe. One helium atom is made of two protons and two neutrons in the nucleus, with two electrons circling around them. Nearly all of the helium in the universe was created during the Big Bang, but helium is also created in stars when hydrogen atoms are fused together and in some radioactive decay processes. About one out of every 10 atoms in the universe is a helium atom.

Helium Atom

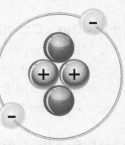

Coulrophobia! Most of the helium we have on Earth comes from the decay of heavy radioactive isotopes, such as uranium. If you go to the circus and a clown gives you a helium balloon, that means someone wearing a disguise has just given you a rubber bag full of radioactive decay products—and your parents are happy about this! Coulrophobia is a fear of clowns. Now you know why.

COSMOLOGY

COSMOLOGY

Try this!

Create your own expanding universe! Get an uninflated party balloon, a ruler, and a pen or a permanent marker. Draw some dots on the balloon, each one about 1/4 inch from the others. When you've drawn a bunch of dots, blow up the balloon and tie it off. Measure how far apart the dots are from one another now. The dots have each moved away from all of the other dots because the space in between them expanded, and the farther away two dots are, the faster they appear to have moved apart from each other.

HUBBLE CONSTANT: Distant galaxies appear to be moving away from the Milky Way, and the farther away they are, the faster they are moving. The Hubble constant relates an object's speed to its distance from Earth. The Hubble constant says that for every megaparsec (19 trillion miles) away something is, its speed increases by 71 kilometers per second, or 150,000 miles per hour.

HUBBLE'S LAW: The law of physics that says the farther a galaxy is from us, the faster it is moving away from us. Because space is expanding equally everywhere in every direction, Hubble's Law is true no matter where in the universe you might be.

HYDROGEN: The smallest type of atom in the universe, and by far the most common. More than 9 out of 10 atoms in the universe is a hydrogen atom. One hydrogen atom is made up of one proton circled by one electron. Hydrogen is the fuel that keeps stars going and provides the light and heat they give off.

Hydrogen Atom

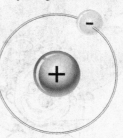

KELVIN: A temperature scale that is often used in science. The Kelvin temperature scale is the same as the Celsius scale, plus 273. So the freezing point of water (0°C) is 273 kelvins, and the boiling point of water (100°C) is 373 kelvins. The coldest possible temperature, called *absolute zero*, is 0 kelvins. The empty space in between galaxies is about 2.7 kelvins, which is -270°C or -455°F.

MASS: A measure of the total amount of matter that makes up an object. The more mass something has, the stronger its gravity is. Mass is different from weight because your mass is a measure of how much matter you are made of, but your weight is a measure of how strongly another object (like the Earth) is pulling on you.

MATTER: Anything that has mass and takes up space. The stuff around you is all made of matter, and so are all objects in space. Light is not matter because it does not have mass or take up space.

True or false? Air is matter.
True! Air is a collection of tiny particles bouncing around. The particles are mostly nitrogen molecules and oxygen molecules, but they all have mass and take up space, so air is matter.

NEUTRINO: A tiny particle with almost no mass. The sun produces an intense stream of neutrinos that passes straight through the Earth at nearly the speed of light without leaving a trace. When the neutrino stream reaches Earth, every square inch of ground is hit by about 420 billion neutrinos per second.

Don't look down! If sunlight passed through the Earth the same way neutrinos do, then during the day sunlight would come from above, and at night sunlight would come up out of the ground.

OBSERVABLE UNIVERSE: The portion of the entire universe that can be seen from Earth. In theory this would go out as far as 46.5 billion light-years away from Earth in every direction, but the most distant object we have been able to see is a galaxy 13.2 billion light-years away.

PROTON: A positively charged subatomic particle that is found in the nucleus of atoms. The number of protons in an atom's nucleus determines which element it is. For example, the lightest element, hydrogen, has only one proton in its nucleus. Helium has two, lithium has three, and so on. Each proton is made of three quarks. (See illustration on p. 7.)

QUARK: A tiny subatomic particle that combines in groups of three to form protons and neutrons. There are six different kinds of quarks, but they are never found individually and are only seen in groups, such as when they form protons and neutrons.

Name that quark! The six different types of quark are called *up, down, top, bottom, strange,* and *charm.* These names are essentially meaningless and don't describe the quarks in any way.

- Up
- Down
- Top
- Bottom
- Strange
- Charm

Up, Up, and ~~Away~~ Down! A proton is made up of two up quarks and one down quark. A neutron is made up of two downs and one up.

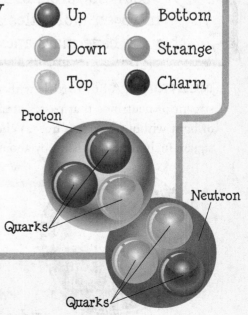

Proton

Quarks

Neutron

Quarks

SPACETIME: In Albert Einstein's theory of relativity, large masses such as black holes not only warp the space around them, but slow down time as well. In this theory space and time are so closely interwoven that they must be considered to be a single concept, called spacetime.

SPEED OF LIGHT: Light travels through space at about 186,282 miles per second (about 670 million miles per hour). This is the fastest speed possible, and anything that has mass can never reach this speed.

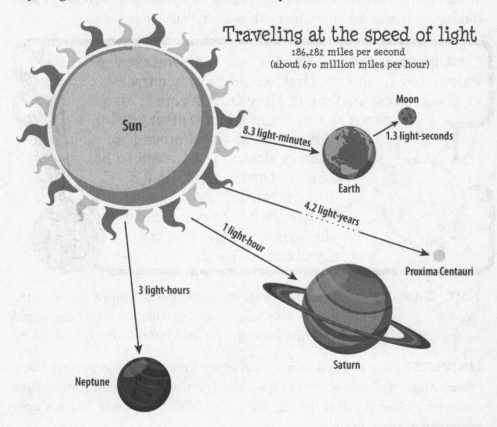

Traveling at the speed of light
186,282 miles per second
(about 670 million miles per hour)

SUBATOMIC PARTICLE: Any particle that is smaller than an atom. The most commonly known subatomic particles are protons, neutrons, and electrons, which are the pieces that every atom is made of.

Subatomic Particles
- ⊕ Protons
- ● Neutrons
- ⊖ Electrons

Cosmology

TEMPERATURE: A measure of how much heat energy is in something. Atoms and molecules are always moving, even in an object that is sitting still. In liquids and gases, the atoms and molecules can move around, but in solid materials, the atoms and molecules vibrate back and forth without moving around. When an object gains more heat energy, its temperature increases and the atoms and molecules it's made of speed up. When an object loses heat energy, its temperature decreases and the atoms and molecules it's made of slow down. The lowest possible temperature is *absolute zero*, where their motion has stopped completely. There is no upper limit to how high temperature can go.

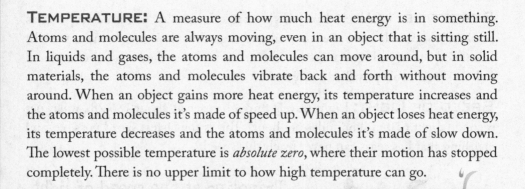

Hot enough for ya? The hottest temperature ever calculated in the universe would have occurred in the briefest instant in time (10^{-43} seconds, also known as one Planck time) after the Big Bang, when the temperature of the explosion is believed to be about 10 thousand billion billion billion (10^{32}) degrees Fahrenheit. For comparison, the surface of the sun is only about 10,000°F.

TIME DILATION: As you enter a strong gravitational field or approach the speed of light, time slows down for you compared to what somebody else would experience. This is called time dilation and is part of Einstein's theory of relativity.

UNIVERSE: Everything that exists, including all matter and energy everywhere. Observations of distant objects in space indicate that the universe formed from a massive explosion called the Big Bang 13.7 billion years ago, and has been expanding in size ever since.

WEIGHT: The force due to gravity that one object applies against another object, such as the force you exert against the ground, or the force a book exerts against a table. Weight depends on the mass of the object and on how strong the gravity is that is acting on the object. Because gravity on the moon is only one-sixth of gravity on Earth, on the moon you would weigh only one-sixth of what you weigh on Earth.

WORMHOLE: A theoretical shortcut through space. Einstein's theory of relativity says that it's possible that two distant points in space could be connected by a tunnel through spacetime that would allow you to get from one place to another almost instantly. Wormholes are often used in science fiction stories as a way to travel great distances through space, but so far no wormholes have ever been seen.

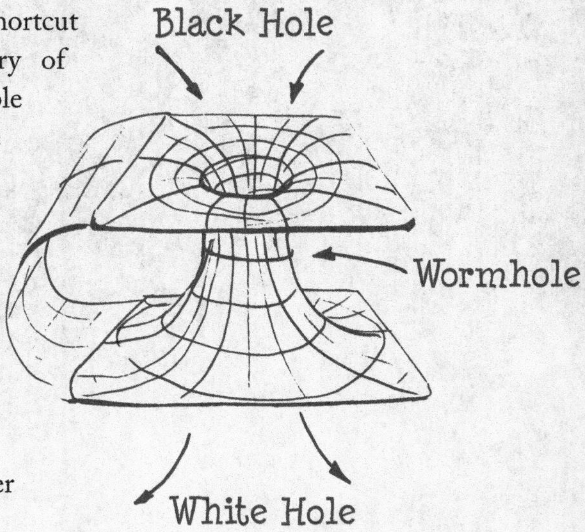

Black Hole

Wormhole

White Hole

Try this!

Get a spaceship that can travel at near the speed of light, and two perfect clocks that are exactly right down to the billionth of a second. Take one clock with you and zoom around the universe at nearly the speed of light for a few years. When you get home, compare the two clocks. The clock that was left at home will be ahead of the clock that you took with you, because while you were traveling at such high speeds, time was passing more slowly for you than it was for the clock on Earth. Try it and see!

COSMOLOGY

15

STARS AND GALAXIES

THE UNIVERSE TODAY

The universe today is a far different place than it was 13.7 billion years ago. Shortly after the Big Bang, the universe was a hot swirl of hydrogen and helium atoms. Today the universe consists of a dazzling variety of objects—stars and planets, galaxies, nebulas, and mysterious black holes to name a few.

Although early astronomers believed stars were eternal and unchanging, we know now that all stars are constantly changing. As stars change, so does the universe itself. Stars take the smallest atoms in the universe—the hydrogen and helium atoms that were created in the Big Bang—and press them together to form larger atoms. Everything around us, from the ground you walk on to the air you breathe to your own body and the book in your hands, is made up of atoms that were created deep inside of stars.

Creating new atoms comes at a terrible cost to stars. Once they've used up the hydrogen in their cores to make larger atoms, stars begin to die. The most massive stars exit the celestial stage as a spectacular supernova, spraying their new atoms into space and then collapsing down to become a tiny neutron star or a black hole. Smaller stars like our sun expand to hundreds of times their original size and shine brighter than they ever have before, and then quietly shrink back down into a white dwarf the size of a planet.

But the end of a large star doesn't mean the end of change, because the atoms that were blown into space in the supernova can swirl together to form a whole new solar system. A smaller star just like our sun can form, orbited by an active family of planets, asteroids, comets, and meteoroids. Stars are forming and dying every day in the universe, bringing about continuous changes in their galaxies.

This chapter contains some of the strangest terms in all of astronomy—words like pulsar, quasar, black hole, magnetar, blazar, along with red giant, blue supergiant, and black dwarf. This is the vocabulary of deep space astronomy—the study of the universe outside of our own solar system.

STARS AND GALAXIES

LIFE CYCLE OF A STAR

(Sizes are not to scale)

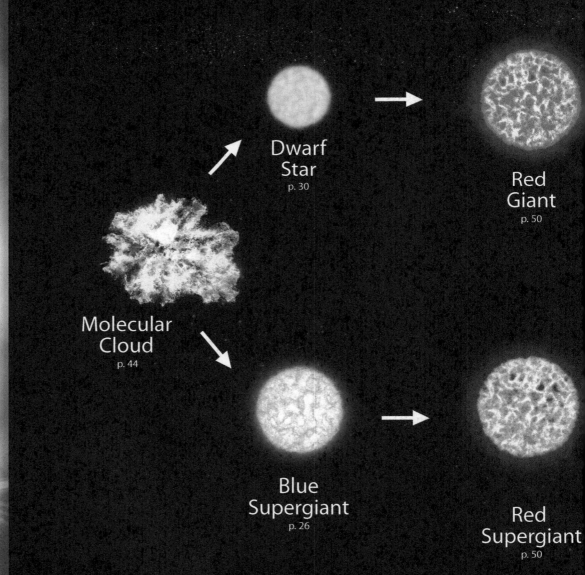

Dwarf
Star
p. 30

Red
Giant
p. 50

Molecular
Cloud
p. 44

Blue
Supergiant
p. 26

Red
Supergiant
p. 50

Planetary
Nebula
p. 46

White
Dwarf
p. 57

Neutron
Star
p. 45

Supernova
p. 54

Black Hole
p. 24

STARS AND GALAXIES

STARS AND GALAXIES

ABSOLUTE MAGNITUDE: A measure of how bright an object in space actually is, rather than how bright it appears. Sometimes one star looks brighter than another because it's closer, even if it's not giving off as much light. Absolute magnitude compares each star's actual brightness.

ABSORPTION LINE: When the light from a distant star passes through a cloud of atoms or molecules on its way to Earth, the atoms or molecules in the cloud absorb some of that light, leaving dark lines in the emission spectrum of the star. Each element has its own absorption "fingerprint," so when the light reaches Earth, we can tell which elements are in the cloud by where the absorption lines appear.

> **Are you Sirius?** Sirius appears to be the brightest star in our night sky (not counting planets), and Canopus looks second brightest, due to absolute magnitude. Canopus actually gives off more than 500 times as much light as Sirius, but Canopus is so much farther away that Sirius appears to be twice as bright as Canopus.

ACCRETION: The process in which small pieces of matter are gradually drawn together by gravity and accumulate to form a larger object such as an asteroid or a planet.

ACCRETION DISK: A flat disk of dust and gas that spins quickly around a black hole or other dense object as it is being sucked in. As the dust and gas in the accretion disk grow closer to the center, the accretion disk heats up and gives off light. The bright nucleus in the center of some galaxies is due to light being given off from the accretion disk around a black hole.

A three-dimensional simulation of an accretion disk.

ACTIVE GALACTIC NUCLEUS: A bright area in the center of some galaxies that is thought to be the area surrounding a supermassive black hole. As matter is drawn into the supermassive black hole, it heats up and gives off more light than the stars do. A galaxy with an active galactic nucleus is called an *active galaxy*.

Sleeping giant. The supermassive black hole (p. 54) in the center of the Milky Way has already eaten everything within its reach and is quiet. If it were still actively eating, the Milky Way would have an active galactic nucleus and our night sky would be much brighter.

ACTIVE GALAXY: A galaxy that has an active galactic nucleus. The core of an active galaxy gives off more light than all of the stars of the galaxy combined. When active galaxies are viewed from the side, we call them radio galaxies. When viewed from an angle, the bright core of an active galaxy outshines the rest of the galaxy and we call it a *quasar*. When viewed directly from above or below, an active galaxy looks like a compact quasar and we call it a *blazar*.

ALPHA CENTAURI: A triple star system that includes *Proxima Centauri*, which is the nearest star to our sun. Proxima Centauri is the dimmest of the three stars that make up Alpha Centauri, and is not visible to the naked eye. Only the other two stars, Alpha Centauri A and Alpha Centauri B, can be seen. Alpha Centauri is the third brightest star in the sky but can only be seen from the Southern Hemisphere in the constellation Centaurus.

Alpha Centauri A and B

Beta Centauri

Proxima Centauri

STARS AND GALAXIES

21

STARS AND GALAXIES

ANDROMEDA GALAXY: The closest galaxy to the Milky Way. It is a spiral galaxy 2.3 million light-years away, and is the most distant thing that can be seen with the naked eye. It appears to us as a dim star in the constellation Andromeda and is best seen on moonless nights. The Andromeda galaxy has about three times as many stars as the Milky Way.

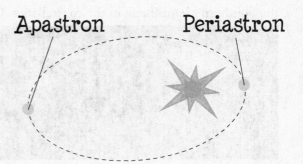

Hey, watch where you're going! The Andromeda Galaxy is on a collision course with the Milky Way. In about 4 billion years, the two galaxies will collide and become one massive elliptical galaxy.

APASTRON: The point in a binary star system where the two stars are farthest apart, or the point where a body orbiting a star is farthest from the star.

Apastron   Periastron

APPARENT MAGNITUDE: A measurement of how bright a star (or other object) looks from Earth. Closer objects can appear brighter even if they're not giving off as much light as a more distant object. Apparent magnitude is also sometimes called *apparent brightness* or *relative magnitude*. (See *Absolute Magnitude*, p. 20.)

Apparent Magnitude Scale

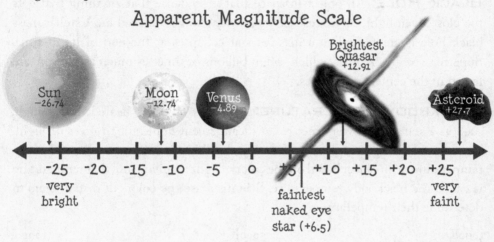

Sun −26.74

Moon −12.74

Venus −4.89

Brightest Quasar +12.91

Asteroid +27.7

−25   −20   −15   −10   −5   0   +5   +10   +15   +20   +25

very bright

faintest naked eye star (+6.5)

very faint

ASTERISM: A group or "picture" of stars that is not a constellation. An asterism might only have stars from one constellation, or be a combination of parts of several constellations. Common examples of asterisms are the Big Dipper (contained entirely within the constellation Ursa Major) and the summer triangle (composed of stars in the constellations Aquila, Lyra, and Cygnus).

BARNARD'S STAR: A red dwarf star about 6 light-years from Earth. It is the closest star in the Northern Hemisphere and is located at a point in the sky that makes it convenient to study, so Barnard's Star is one of the most-studied stars. Like all red dwarfs, it is too small and dim to be seen with the naked eye.

BINARY STAR: A system of two stars that orbit a common center. Usually one star is brighter than the other, and is called the *primary star*. The dimmer star is called the *secondary* or *companion star*. A system with more than two stars is called a *multiple star system*. More than half of the stars visible in the night sky are believed to be binary stars, but to the naked eye they each appear as single stars.

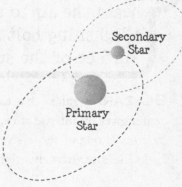

Secondary Star

Primary Star

STARS AND GALAXIES

23

BLACK DWARF: The final end of a dwarf star. A star like our sun that does not have enough mass to explode as a supernova eventually shrinks down to a white dwarf, and after billions of years when it has cooled to the point where it no longer gives off heat and light, it becomes a black dwarf.

BLACK HOLE: An object in space that is so dense that anything that gets too close, even light, cannot escape its gravity and gets sucked in. A stellar mass black hole is created when a massive star collapses at the end of its lifetime. Supermassive black holes, which weigh billions of times as much as the sun, are found in the centers of galaxies.

BLACKBODY TEMPERATURE: When as object is heated hot enough, such as a star or a stove burner or an incandescent light bulb, it gives off light. The color of the light depends on how hot the object is. When you determine the temperature of an object based on the color of light it's giving off, that temperature is called the blackbody temperature. Scientists use the colors of distant stars to determine their temperatures.

1000K   5000K   10000K

Blackbody Temperature

Which is hotter, a lightning bolt or the sun?
A lightning bolt! You can't find the temperature of a lightning bolt using a thermometer, but by measuring the color of the light given off, scientists have determined that lightning heats the air to more than 50,000°F, making a lightning bolt five times hotter than the surface of the sun.

BLAZAR: A galaxy that has an actively feeding supermassive black hole in the center gives off intense streams of radiation directed upward and downward from its core. If one of those streams of radiation is aimed toward Earth, the galaxy looks like an extremely bright, compact quasar, and we call it a blazar.

Black Hole FAQ

Q: How big is a black hole?

A: Nobody knows! We can estimate the mass of a black hole, but there's no way to know its actual size. A black hole could be the size of a city, or it could be smaller than a pinpoint in space, but we have no way of knowing. All we can say for sure is that it's smaller than its event horizon (p. 30; also known as its Schwarzschild radius, p. 51).

Q: Okay then, how massive is a black hole?

A: Most black holes are one of two types: stellar black holes or supermassive black holes. A stellar mass black hole is formed when a giant star goes supernova (p. 54) and its core collapses into a sphere that weighs usually about 5-10 times as much as our sun. The supermassive black holes in the center of galaxies normally weigh billions of times as much as our sun. Nobody knows how supermassive black holes are formed. There's a big gap between 10 times the mass of the sun and a billion times the mass of the sun, but we have found very few black holes that fall into that intermediate range. Nobody knows how those are formed.

Q: If not even light can escape from a black hole, why do I see pictures of black holes giving off light?

A: The black hole itself doesn't give off light. The black hole draws gas and dust into it, and as that material gets closer to the black hole it gives off energy in the form of light. The closer it gets the brighter it glows, and so the light you see is from material that is outside of the black hole's event horizon. Once the gas and dust reach the event horizon, their light is trapped by the black hole. The material could still be falling toward the black hole and glowing brighter than ever, but that light never escapes the black hole, so nobody knows for sure.

STARS AND GALAXIES

Black Hole FAQ

Q: For a FAQ, you sure say "nobody knows" a lot.
A: Well nobody does. Besides, that's not a question.

Q: Why doesn't anybody know these things?
A: We usually learn about objects in space by studying the light (or the electromagnetic radiation such as X-rays or radio waves) they give off. Objects that don't give off light usually reflect light that comes from other sources, and we can learn about them that way. You could say that all of the information we get from outer space is carried to us by light. But a black hole doesn't give off or reflect light, and therefore provides no information. It's like a bottomless pit that information falls into but never comes out of. In 2016, astronomers announced they have successfully measured gravitational waves (p. 9) for the first time. Gravitational waves might one day provide a new way to learn more about black holes.

BLUE SUPERGIANT: The brightest and hottest type of star. A blue supergiant typically has a mass that is 10–100 times that of the sun, but they burn through their fuel faster than any other type of star. A blue supergiant can have a lifetime of less than a million years, compared with our sun's expected lifetime of about 10 billion years. Rigel, which is the second-brightest star in the constellation Orion, is a blue supergiant.

Rigel
Blue Supergiant

Arcturus
Red Giant

Sun

BROWN DWARF: An object in space that is larger than a planet, but smaller than a star. Most brown dwarfs are only slightly larger in size than Jupiter, but are anywhere from 10 to 80 times heavier. Brown dwarfs give off heat energy but do not shine with visible light the way stars do.

CARBON STAR: An old star that is running out of fuel and has started cooling off. Carbon stars have unusually high levels of carbon in their atmospheres, which give them a deep red color. Most red giants are carbon stars.

CATACLYSMIC VARIABLE STAR: A star that shines brightly for a brief period, then goes back to normal until the next time it shines brightly again. A cataclysmic variable star is actually a close binary star system made up of a normal star and a white dwarf. As gravity from the very dense white dwarf pulls gases away from the surface of the normal star, the gases heat up and give off bright light. In an especially bright cataclysmic variable star, the material taken by the white dwarf can be fused into helium to give off even more energy. This kind of cataclysmic variable star during its bright phase is called a *nova*.

CEPHEID VARIABLE STAR: A star that pulses brighter and dimmer at regular intervals. Cepheid variable stars are like measuring sticks in astronomy, because astronomers can tell how far away a Cepheid variable star is from Earth based on its brightness and how quickly it goes through a bright and dim cycle. They can then use this information to estimate how far away other distant stars and galaxies are.

CHANDRASEKHAR LIMIT: The maximum mass of a white dwarf, about 1.44 times the mass of the sun. Anything larger than this has too much gravity and will collapse into a neutron star or black hole.

STARS AND GALAXIES

COLLAPSAR: Short for "collapsed star," a collapsar is the core of a star after it has exhausted all its fuel and died. A collapsar can be a white dwarf, a neutron star, or a black hole.

COLOR INDEX: A system for classifying stars based on their color and temperature. A star with a lower color index is bluer and hotter than a star with a higher color index, which is redder and cooler.

Star Temperature (K)	Star Color	Star Temperature (K)	Star Color
2,000–3,000		6,000–10,000	
3,000–4,000		10,000–20,000	
4,000–6,000		20,000–30,000	

CYGNUS X-1: The first black hole ever discovered. Cygnus X-1 was first discovered in 1964 as an unknown object giving off X-rays. In 1971 it was determined that it has a mass almost 15 times as much as the sun, but is far too small to be a star, meaning it can only be a stellar mass black hole. Its event horizon has a diameter of about 54 miles (88 km).

DARK NEBULA: A cloud of gas and dust that does not give off any light. We can only see it because it blocks the light coming from stars that are behind it, creating a patch of sky without stars. Dark nebulae are normally visible only through telescopes.

Black beauty! The Horsehead Nebula is a dark nebula composed of dust and non-luminous gas whose shape is outlined by red light from emission nebula IC 434. It is located in the constellation Orion.

DEEP-SKY OBJECT: An object outside the solar system, usually a galaxy, nebula, or star cluster.

DEEP SPACE: Outer space beyond our solar system. Deep space astronomy is the study of distant objects such as other stars and galaxies. Deep space astronomy is one of the main branches of astronomy along with planetary astronomy, which is the study of objects within our solar system.

DEUTERIUM: Most hydrogen atoms are made up of one proton and one electron, but deuterium is a version of hydrogen that has a neutron along with a proton in its nucleus. Deuterium is sometimes called heavy hydrogen.

DOUBLE STAR: Sometimes the term *double star* is used to mean a *binary star*, but it can also mean two stars that appear to be very close together in the sky, even if one is actually much farther away from Earth than the other.

DWARF GALAXY: A small, dim galaxy that is usually found orbiting a larger galaxy. The Milky Way contains 200–400 billion stars, but a typical dwarf galaxy may contain only a few billion stars. Dwarf galaxies may be the leftover pieces resulting from collisions between full-size galaxies, and are often found orbiting large galaxies.

Milky White and the 20 Dwarves? The Milky Way galaxy is orbited by at least 20 dwarf galaxies. The best known of these are the Large Magellanic Cloud and the Small Magellanic Cloud (p. 41).

STARS AND GALAXIES

DWARF STAR: Stars are classified as dwarf, giant, or supergiant. The vast majority are dwarf stars, also known as *main sequence stars*. At least three-fourths of the stars in the Milky Way are red dwarfs, and there are many orange dwarfs as well. Our sun is a yellow dwarf. Not all dwarfs in space are stars: Brown dwarfs are balls of gas that are too small to become stars, and white dwarfs and black dwarfs are the remains of dead stars.

ELLIPTICAL GALAXY: A galaxy that is shaped like a squashed or stretched sphere. Elliptical galaxies are usually made of old, dim stars, and don't have much dust and gas in them for forming new stars.

Hubble Sequence–Classification of Elliptical Galaxies

E0 E1 E2 E3 E4 E5 E6 E7

EMBRYONIC STAR CLOUD: See *Nebula*, p. 44.

EMISSION NEBULA: A cloud of interstellar gas that has been heated up by a nearby star so much that it emits colorful light. This usually happens either when a new star has just formed and is heating the nebula it was born from, or when a dying star throws off its outer layer and creates a nebula around itself, which is then heated by the core of the star that created it.

EVENT HORIZON: The region in space surrounding a black hole from which nothing, not even light, can escape the black hole's gravity. The event horizon is considered the point of no return because anything that reaches the event horizon gets sucked into the black hole. The greater the mass of the black hole, the larger the event horizon is. The event horizon is also called the *Schwarzchild radius*.

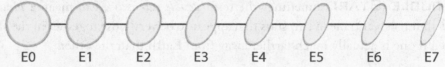

Light is pulled in

Light is trapped in orbit

Event Horizon

Light escapes

EVOLVED STAR: A star that is almost at the end of its life. Most stars evolve to become red giants before either collapsing into white dwarfs or exploding as supernovas.

EXTRAGALACTIC: Outside of the Milky Way.

FUSION: A process in which two or more atoms are pressed together to form one larger atom. This process gives off large amounts of energy. The heat and light from the sun come from the fusion of hydrogen atoms into helium in the core of the sun.

GALACTIC CENTER: The bright central part of a galaxy. The galactic center is small compared to the rest of the galaxy, and usually contains a supermassive black hole. The galactic center is sometimes called the *galactic nucleus*.

Galactic Center

Galactic Disk

GALACTIC DISK: Some types of galaxies, such as the Milky Way, are shaped like a flat circle. In these galaxies, the galactic disk is the visible region that contains all of the stars, planets, gases, and dust that make up the galaxy.

GALAXY: A collection of billions of stars that are held together in a group by gravity. Our galaxy is called the Milky Way and contains anywhere from 200–400 billion stars. Galaxies that contain a few billion stars or less are called *dwarf galaxies*.

Giant Space Frisbee™! The Milky Way is spinning around its center and moving through space at about 1.3 million miles per hour.

STARS AND GALAXIES

31

STARS AND GALAXIES

GALAXY CLUSTER: A collection of galaxies that are moving together through space. A galaxy cluster can have anywhere from about a dozen galaxies to thousands. The Milky Way is in a galaxy cluster called the *local group*. The local group contains at least 54 galaxies, although most of them are dwarf galaxies. The only other major galaxy in the local group is Andromeda.

GALAXY SUPERCLUSTER: A collection of galaxy clusters. The Milky Way is part of a galaxy cluster called the local group, and the local group is part a supercluster called *Laniakea*. Laniakea contains 300–500 galaxy clusters stretched out across 520 million light-years in space.

GASEOUS NEBULA: A thin cloud of gas in space that can be up to hundreds of light-years across. New stars are born when the gases in a nebula are swirl together into denser regions that then draw more gases toward them. Once the process starts, it takes about 10 million years to form a star the size of our sun.

GENERATION OF STARS: A first generation star is one that formed from the material left over from the Big Bang. After a first generation star lives out its life and explodes as a supernova, a new star can form from the remains of the first generation star: This is a second generation star. Our sun is a third-generation star. Each prior generation of star had to die by supernova in order to form a subsequent generation.

How do we know? How do we know the sun is a third generation star? The Big Bang created a universe made up of only the smallest of the atoms: hydrogen, helium, and a little bit of lithium. Stars press small atoms together to create larger ones. This process is called *fusion*, and is how a star gets its energy. Our sun contains larger atoms that it could not have formed on its own, and based on which atoms it contains and in what amounts, astronomers believe it took two previous generations of stars to create all of the heavier atoms that are found in our sun.

GIANT MOLECULAR CLOUD: A large cloud of dust and gas molecules in space. Stars can form inside giant molecular clouds, so a giant molecular cloud can be the beginnings of a star cluster. Giant molecular clouds are a lot like nebulas, but not as hot, so the atoms and ions are able to come together to form molecules.

GIANT STAR: Stars are classified as dwarf, giant, or supergiant. A giant star is much larger than a typical dwarf star like the sun. Dwarf stars evolve into giant stars once they have used up the hydrogen in their core. At that point they begin to cool off and expand up to a hundred times their normal size. When our sun eventually becomes a red giant, it will grow so large it might swallow Earth.

Three and out! Our sun has a parent and a grandparent, but its great-grandparent was the Big Bang itself. Our sun will never have a child star, because our sun is too small to supernova (p. 54) when it dies. Instead the leftover material from our burnt-out sun will collapse into a white dwarf (p. 57).

GLOBULAR CLUSTER: A spherical group of stars tightly bound together by gravity. Globular clusters are typically made up of hundreds of thousands of very old stars. The Milky Way has at least 150 globular clusters all orbiting the core of the galaxy. The stars in a globular cluster are up to 1,000 times closer to one another than other stars in the galaxy are, and are so close their gravity interactions prevent them from having any planets.

STARS AND GALAXIES

HAWKING RADIATION: Black holes can create light and particles from energy near their event horizon, and emit these into space. The light and particles that are emitted are called Hawking radiation. If a black hole is not actively feeding on surrounding matter, Hawking radiation can cause the black hole to lose mass and energy. In that case, the black hole slowly evaporates and shrinks over time, and this can ultimately lead to the shrinking black hole heating up and exploding.

HERTZSPRUNG-RUSSELL (H-R) DIAGRAM: By looking at only the brightness and color of a star, astronomers can tell what kind of star it is and where it is in its lifetime. A graph of the brightness of a star versus its color is called

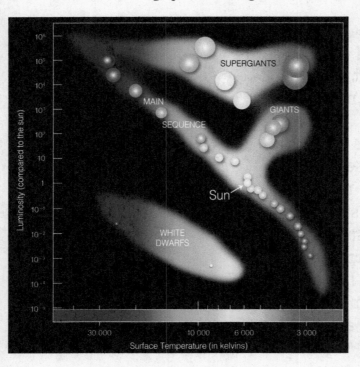

an H-R diagram. The color and temperature are related—the more red a star is, the colder it is and the bluer a star is, the hotter it is. Cool, dim stars are in the lower right end of the main sequence and hot, bright stars are in the upper left. Stars fall into three categories on an H-R diagram: the diagonal line through the middle is known as the main sequence, and stars on this line (called *main sequence stars* or *dwarf stars*) fuse hydrogen as fuel. Ninety percent of all known stars are main sequence stars. The stars near the top of the diagram are the giants and supergiants. These are larger and brighter than dwarf stars, and fuse elements other than hydrogen (usually helium). White dwarfs, near the bottom of the H-R diagram, are the still hot remains of dead stars that have used up all their fuel, and give off heat and light as they gradually cool off.

Biography of our sun. The line on this H-R diagram traces the evolution of our sun over its entire lifetime, all the way to its death. Our sun began as a cloud of gas and dust left over from a supernova. This gas and dust formed into a yellow dwarf star 4.6 billion years ago, and that's what the sun has been ever since.

In another 4.5 billion years the sun will have used up the hydrogen in its core. At this point, the sun begins to cool off, expand in size, and grow brighter. It becomes brighter because it now has much more surface area—our sun is becoming a red giant. This is where the line on the graph leaves the main sequence and moves toward the area labeled "Red Giant." As a red giant, the sun is fusing helium instead of hydrogen.

As the sun goes through various phases of burning different fuels, its brightness and temperature fluctuate—this is where the line on the H-R diagram zigzags back and forth. When the sun runs out of helium, it can't fuse any higher elements. When this happens, the sun sheds its outer layer and becomes a planetary nebula—a hot core of a sun that is no longer fusing elements, surrounded by a cloud of gases.

Because the core is no longer fusing atoms together, gravity causes it to collapse in on itself. This collapse heats up the sun's core tremendously—the line on the diagram goes all the way off scale to the left because the collapsed core grows much hotter than this graph can show. The sun's core is not a white dwarf. Because the white dwarf is not fusing elements, it is not generating any heat and eventually cools down.

All stars go through an evolutionary path over the course of their lifetime that can be tracked on an H-R diagram.

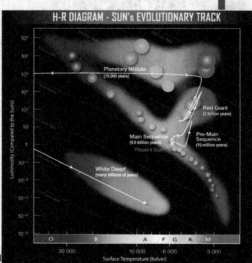

H-R DIAGRAM - SUN's EVOLUTIONARY TRACK

Planetary Nebula (10,000 years)

Red Giant (2 billion years)

Main Sequence (9.5 billion years)

Pre-Main Sequence (10 million years)

Present Sun

White Dwarf (many billions of years)

Luminosity (Compared to the Sun's)

Surface Temperature (Kelvin)

STARS AND GALAXIES

STARS AND GALAXIES

HUBBLE DEEP FIELD (HDF): An image taken by the Hubble Space Telescope in 1995 that showed what was at the time the most distant objects ever photographed. The Hubble Deep Field shows more than 3,000 objects in space, nearly all of them distant galaxies. Because they are so far away, the image shows the galaxies as they would have appeared 12 billion years ago.

HUBBLE ULTRA-DEEP FIELD (UDF): An image released in 2004 that goes even deeper into space than the Hubble Deep Field does. The Hubble Ultra-Deep Field shows more than 10,000 young galaxies in space as they would have appeared 13 billion years ago.

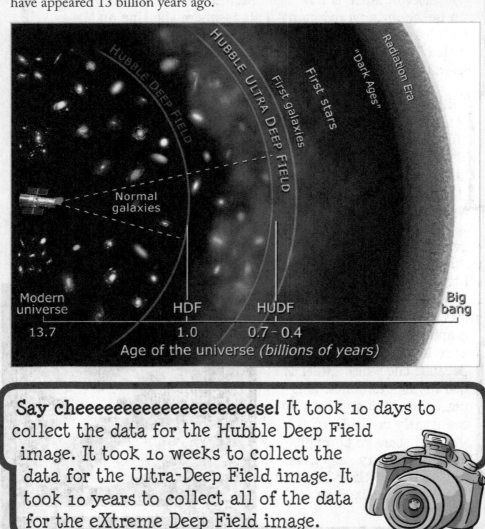

Normal galaxies

HUBBLE DEEP FIELD

HUBBLE ULTRA DEEP FIELD

First galaxies

First stars

"Dark Ages"

Radiation Era

Modern universe	HDF	HUDF	Big bang
13.7	1.0	0.7 - 0.4	

Age of the universe *(billions of years)*

Say cheeeeeeeeeeeeeeeeeeese! It took 10 days to collect the data for the Hubble Deep Field image. It took 10 weeks to collect the data for the Ultra-Deep Field image. It took 10 years to collect all of the data for the eXtreme Deep Field image.

HUBBLE EXTREME DEEP FIELD (XDF): An image from the Hubble Space Telescope released in 2012 that is farthest out we have ever seen in space. The XDF includes more than 15,000 distant galaxies dating back to about 13.2 billion years, or just 500 million years after the Big Bang. The galaxies in the XDF are all very young galaxies, so the XDF provides information about how galaxies first formed billions of years ago.

HYDROSTATIC EQUILIBRIUM: The gravity of a star pulls all of its material inward, and the pressure created by the fusion reactions in the star's core push the star's material outward. When the inward pull of gravity is equal to the outward push of the pressure, the star has a stable size and is said to be at hydrostatic equilibrium.

True or false? The sun will always be the same size it is today.

False! As our sun grows older, the pressure from the fusion reactions in its core will increase, and the sun will expand as a red giant (p. 50) past the orbit of Venus and possibly all of the way to Earth.

Then when the sun's fuel is exhausted, the pressure will drop and the sun's gravity will pull the sun into a white dwarf (p. 57) that is about the size of Earth—less than one-millionth of the sun's current size.

HYPERGALAXY: A large spiral galaxy that is orbited by several small elliptical galaxies. Our Milky Way and the neighboring Andromeda galaxy are both hypergalaxies.

STARS AND GALAXIES

INTERACTING GALAXIES: Two or more galaxies that are so close that they overlap. Sometimes the two galaxies combine to form a single, larger galaxy, and sometimes they pass through each other. When two galaxies pass through each other, the gravitational pull they exert on one another during the interaction leaves both galaxies stretched and distorted from their original shape, and can pull away small regions of stars to form new dwarf galaxies.

Far, far away. These four interacting galaxies (NGC 7319, 7318A, 7318B, and 7317) are about 280 million light-years from Earth.

INTERGALACTIC: Refers to the space between galaxies.

INTERSTELLAR: Refers to the space between stars within a single galaxy.

INTERSTELLAR DUST: Small particles of matter in the space between stars that isn't part of a larger cloud such as a nebula.

INTERSTELLAR MEDIUM: The gas and random dust particles in the empty space between stars that isn't part of a nebula or other large cloud. The interstellar medium includes interstellar dust as well as atoms, ions, electrons, and molecules.

ION: In chemistry, an ion is an atom or molecule that has lost or gained one or more electrons, and therefore has a positive or negative charge. In astronomy, nearly all ions are hydrogen atoms that have lost an electron. A mixture of ions and free electrons is called *plasma*. Most of the matter we see in the universe is in the form of plasma.

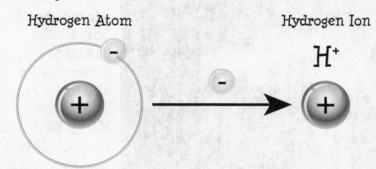

Hydrogen Atom

Hydrogen Ion

H^+

IRREGULAR GALAXY: Most galaxies are shaped like either flat disks or elliptical clouds in space. Irregular galaxies are shaped like chaotic blobs. Often this is due to a past interaction with another galaxy that distorted the galaxy from its original shape.

JET: Very dense objects such as black holes often emit high-energy streams of electrically charged matter (mostly protons and electrons) from their north and south poles or from the accretion disk around the object. These sprays of matter, which sometimes travel at close to the speed of light, are called *jets*. Astronomers don't fully understand how jets are formed.

Milkomeda? In about 4 billion years the Milky Way and Andromeda are expected to collide. Each galaxy has so much empty space that the stars themselves won't crash into each other, but the combined gravity of the two galaxies will cause them to merge into one large elliptical galaxy (p. 30) that has been nicknamed Milkomeda.

STARS AND GALAXIES

Stars and Galaxies

LANIAKEA: The galaxy supercluster that contains the Milky Way. The Laniakea Supercluster stretches more than 520 million light-years and contains more than 100,000 galaxies grouped into 300–500 galaxy clusters. Laniakea is Hawaiian for "immeasurable heaven."

Milky Way

Home sweet home. The Laniakea Supercluster is home to our galaxy, the Milky Way, and 100,000 other nearby galaxies.

LENTICULAR GALAXY: A flat, circular galaxy that doesn't have a spiral structure like the Milky Way does. A lenticular galaxy looks like an elliptical galaxy that has been squashed flat. Just like elliptical galaxies, lenticular galaxies are made up almost completely of older stars, and very few new stars are forming there.

LIGHT-YEAR: The distance light can travel in a vacuum in one year. One light-year is almost 6 trillion miles: 5,878,499,810,000 miles to be exact, or 9,460,528,400,000 kilometers.

Speedy delivery! Alpha Centauri, the closest star system to our sun, is a triple star that is about 4.5 light-years away from Earth. When you look up and see light from Alpha Centauri, that light has been traveling through outer space for almost 4.5 years before it reaches your eye.

4.5 light-years = 26,000,000,000,000 miles

Alpha Centauri

LOCAL GROUP: Galaxies are not evenly distributed in the universe, and instead tend to be found in clusters. The cluster that contains the Milky Way is known as the local group. The Milky Way and Andromeda are by far the two largest galaxies in the local group. There are a total of about 54 galaxies in the local group. Almost all of them are dwarf galaxies.

LUMINOSITY: The total amount of energy given off by a star in one second. Luminosity depends on the size of the star and the color or temperature of the star. Luminosity increases as size increases, and also increases as the surface temperature of the star increases (or as the color shifts from red toward blue).

MAGELLANIC CLOUDS: The Large and Small Magellanic Clouds are two dwarf galaxies that orbit the Milky Way. They both look like they were once spiral galaxies, but gravity from the Milky Way has deformed them and turned them into irregular galaxies. The Magellanic Clouds are visible to the naked eye in the Southern Hemisphere.

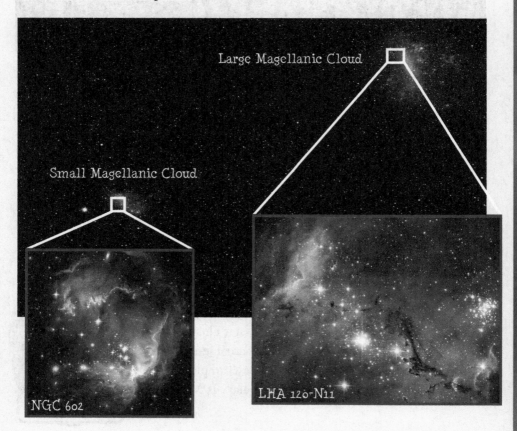

Large Magellanic Cloud

Small Magellanic Cloud

NGC 602

LHA 120-N11

MAGNETAR: A special type of neutron star that has a powerful magnetic field. The magnetic field causes the magnetar to give off high energy X-rays and gamma rays. The magnetic field of a magnetar decays after about 10,000 years, and then the energy emissions stop. At that point the magnetar is like a regular neutron star.

Magnetic personality! This is an artist's impression of a magnetar with a magnetic loop.

MAIN SEQUENCE: The diagonal line of stars on a Hertzsprung-Russel diagram that shows stars getting bigger and brighter as they get hotter. Main sequence stars are normal, healthy stars that are fusing hydrogen to helium in their cores. All main sequence stars are dwarf stars. Stars that are not in the main sequence in the H-R diagram have either run out of hydrogen in their core and entered the last part of their life, or are already dead.

MEGAPARSEC: A distance equal to a million parsecs, or about 3.26 million light-years. Megaparsecs are usually used to measure distances too big to even use light-years, such as the distance between galaxies or galaxy clusters.

MESSIER CATALOG: A list of deep sky objects that was first compiled by Charles Messier in 1771 and was expanded upon until 1960, resulting in a total of 110 objects. The Messier catalog includes many nebulas, star clusters, and galaxies that are visible from the Northern Hemisphere, each identified with an M-number. For example, M1 is the Crab Nebula, and the Andromeda galaxy is M31.

Charles Messier, c. 1770

STARS AND GALAXIES

MESSIER OBJECT: An object in deep space that is included in the Messier catalog.

MILKY WAY: The spiral galaxy that contains our solar system. The Milky Way is estimated to contain about 200–400 billion stars, although it may contain as many as one trillion stars. Our sun is located on one of the spiral arms about halfway out from the center of the Milky Way. In the center of the Milky Way is a supermassive black hole that weighs more than four million times as much as our sun.

Why don't we know? The reason it's so hard to know exactly how many stars are in the Milky Way is that most stars are red dwarfs (p. 49), which give off very little light and also have very little mass, and therefore very little gravity. This makes them hard to detect when they're far away. The Milky Way could contain hundreds of millions of red dwarfs that we don't know about.

MILLISECOND PULSAR: An ordinary pulsar will rotate on its axis once every 1–10 seconds, but a millisecond pulsar spins around on its axis hundreds of times each second. Most millisecond pulsars are very old neutron stars that have accreted new matter over long periods of time. Adding mass caused them to spin faster.

Let me off! The fastest-spinning pulsar (p. 48) discovered so far rotates on its axis 716 times in one second!

STARS AND GALAXIES

MOLECULAR CLOUD: A molecular cloud is a special kind of nebula. It is more dense and not as hot as a typical nebula, and this allows hydrogen atoms in the cloud to come together to form hydrogen molecules. Molecular clouds do not give off light the way nebulas do, but because the material in them is closer together, molecular clouds are likely places for new stars to form.

Maternity ward! The Eagle Nebula is a molecular cloud where new stars are gradually forming. The different colors are due to ions of different atoms. In this image sulfur ions show up as red, hydrogen ions as green, and oxygen ions as blue.

MULTIPLE STAR: Often times what looks like one star in the sky is really two or more stars that orbit each other in space. They're so close together that to us they look like one bright star. Alpha Centauri, the third brightest star in the sky, is really a three-star system.

NEBULA: A massive cloud of gas and dust in space, so large that it can create thousands of stars and solar systems. Some nebulas are regions in a galaxy where new stars are currently being formed, and other nebulas are the scattered leftovers of exploded stars, which can eventually be used to form new stars.

Sheer beauty! The Veil Nebula is spread out over such a vast distance in space that it takes up 36 times as much area in the sky as the full moon does.

NEUTRON STAR: The collapsed core of a star that was too large to become a white dwarf but too small to become a black hole. Neutron stars are only about 10 miles in diameter but can have a mass up to three times as much as the sun. Neutron stars are made up almost entirely of neutrons. Pulsars and magnetars are special types of neutron stars.

Neutron Star

Mass
1.5–3 times the Sun

Diameter
~10 miles

Solid Crust
~1 mile thick

Heavy Liquid Interior
Mostly neutrons,
with other particles

Small but heavy. One teaspoon of a neutron star would weigh 100 million tons. The only thing in the universe that is more dense than a neutron star is a black hole.

NGC: NGC stands for the New General Catalogue, which is the most comprehensive list of objects in deep space. The NGC contains 7,840 objects, which are known as NGC objects. Each object has its own identification number. For example, the Crab Nebula is NGC 1952, and the Andromeda galaxy is NGC 224. The NGC identification number is based on the position of the object in the sky.

NOVA: A star that goes through cycles of being very bright and very dim. Often the dim phase is not visible to the naked eye, so the bright phase looks like a new star in the sky. The word *nova* is Latin for "new."

NUCLEAR FUSION: See *Fusion*, p. 31.

GK Persei
(Nova Persei 1901)

STARS AND GALAXIES

45

STARS AND GALAXIES

Why does it do that? Novas (p. 45) actually binary star systems (p. 23) in which a white dwarf (p. 57) is pulling hydrogen from the surface of its companion star. When the white dwarf has accumulated enough hydrogen from its companion, it flares up in a burst of fusion (p. 31) that gives off bright light. As that fuel is used up, the white dwarf grows dim until it accumulates enough hydrogen for another burst of fusion.

OPEN CLUSTER: A collection of a thousand or so stars that formed together from the same molecular cloud. Open clusters are found in the disks of spiral galaxies and in irregular galaxies.

PARSEC: A distance equal to 3.26 light-years, or about 19 trillion miles.

PLANETARY NEBULA: A cloud of gas and dust that surrounds a dead or dying star. There are no planets in a planetary nebula, but when the first one was discovered in the 1780s, the nebula resembled planets around a star, and the name has stuck.

NGC 7293, the Helix Nebula, is a planetary nebula.

PLASMA: Normally on Earth we encounter matter as either a solid, a liquid, or a gas, but at extremely high temperatures, atoms can be stripped of some or all of their electrons. The result of this is a hot swirl of negatively charged electrons and positively charged particles called *ions*. This mixture of ions and electrons is called *plasma*. Most of the observable matter of the universe, including the outer layers of stars, is in the form of plasma.

Hot blooded? Blood contains a liquid that is also called plasma, but don't let the name confuse you. Blood plasma is mostly water with some dissolved proteins and minerals in it and is nothing at all like the plasma in space.

PROTOGALAXY: A vast cloud made up almost entirely of hydrogen and helium that is condensing to form the beginnings of a galaxy.

PROTOSTAR: A cloud of gas and dust that is in the process of collapsing into a star.

PROXIMA CENTAURI: The nearest star to our sun. It is part of the triple star system of *Alpha Centauri*. Proxima Centauri itself is a red dwarf that is too dim to be seen with the naked eye, but its two yellow dwarf companion stars (Alpha Centauri A and Alpha Cantauri B) appear as the third brightest star in the night sky but is only visible in the Southern Hemisphere.

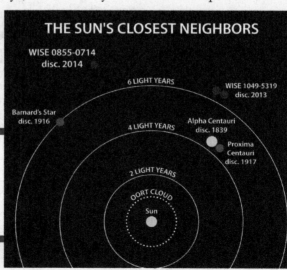

THE SUN'S CLOSEST NEIGHBORS

WISE 0855-0714
disc. 2014

6 LIGHT YEARS

WISE 1049-5319
disc. 2013

Barnard's Star
disc. 1916

4 LIGHT YEARS

Alpha Centauri
disc. 1839

Proxima
Centauri
disc. 1917

2 LIGHT YEARS

OORT CLOUD

Sun

Hi neighbors! Proxima Centauri is 4.24 light-years away from Earth.

STARS AND GALAXIES

PULSAR: A special type of neutron star that emits a powerful beam of radio waves. The beam shoots straight out into space, and as the pulsar rotates, the beam sweeps across space like a lighthouse beacon. Most pulsars rotate on their axis 1–10 times per second, so from Earth the pulsar looks like a rapidly flashing radio signal in space. Although most pulsars emit radio waves, some emit different forms of electromagnetic radiation such as visible light.

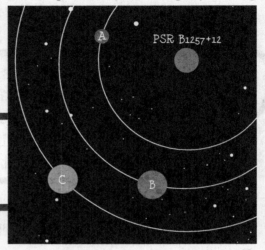

PSR B1257+12

I used to be a star! This pulsar, named PSR B1257+12, in the constellation Virgo has at least three planets.

QUASAR: The brightest objects in the universe. A galaxy that has an actively feeding supermassive black hole in the center gives off intense streams of radiation directed upward and downward from its core. If we are viewing an active galaxy from a tilted angle, we can see the bright glow coming off the galactic core that surrounds the black hole. This glow is so bright it outshines all of the stars in the galaxy. One quasar can give off 100 times as much light as our entire galaxy.

We'll name the baby "Quasar"! When they were first discovered, quasars were called *quasi-stellar radio sources*, which means "something that's kind of like a star, but is giving off radio waves." Quasi-stellar radio source was shortened to quasar, and even though we now know that quasars are nothing at all like stars, the name has stuck.

RADIO GALAXY: A galaxy that has an actively feeding supermassive black hole in the center gives off intense streams of radiation directed upward and downward from its core, and is called an *active galaxy*. If we are viewing an active galaxy from the side, we can see both jets of radiation, and we call that a radio galaxy. The jets form massive plumes of dust and gas in space. The core of a radio galaxy gives off a bright light, but it doesn't appear bright to us because that light is partially blocked by the accretion disk around the supermassive black hole.

Dwarfing a giant galaxy! The jets and plumes from Hercules A, a supergiant elliptical radio galaxy, are more than a million light-years long!

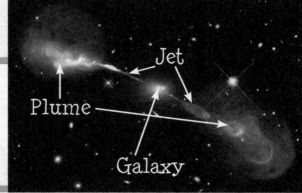

Jet

Plume

Galaxy

RED DWARF: The smallest, coolest, and dimmest kind of star. Red dwarf stars range from less than one tenth the size of the sun to half the size of the sun. Red dwarfs are the most common type of star in the universe: About three-fourths of the stars in the solar neighborhood are red dwarfs, but all of them are too small and dim to be seen with the naked eye. The nearest star to the sun, Proxima Centauri, is a red dwarf.

Watching the universe go by. Red dwarf stars live longer than any other type of star. They burn their fuel so slowly that their life expectancy is longer than the current age of the universe. That means some of the first stars that formed after the Big Bang could still be burning today, and could continue to burn long after our sun has died!

STARS AND GALAXIES

STARS AND GALAXIES

RED GIANT: A star that has fused all of the hydrogen in its core, and now only has a thin shell of hydrogen surrounding a helium core. Most red giants have less mass than the sun, but are 20–100 times larger. Because red giants have so much surface area giving off light they can be several hundred times brighter than the sun. When our sun has consumed all of the hydrogen in its core it will become a red giant.

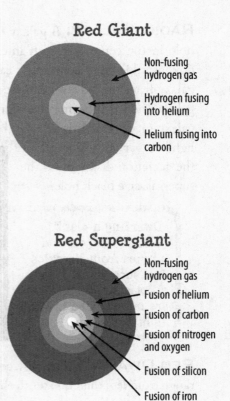

Red Giant

Non-fusing hydrogen gas

Hydrogen fusing into helium

Helium fusing into carbon

RED SUPERGIANT: Red supergiants, like red giants, are stars that have fused all of the helium in their cores. Supergiants develop from bigger stars than giants do, usually stars between 10 and 40 times the mass of the sun. Supergiants are defined by their brightness rather than their size, so supergiant stars are not always bigger than giant stars, but they are always brighter—up to hundreds of thousands times brighter than the sun.

Red Supergiant

Non-fusing hydrogen gas

Fusion of helium

Fusion of carbon

Fusion of nitrogen and oxygen

Fusion of silicon

Fusion of iron

RING GALAXY: A galaxy that consists of a bright center surrounded by a large ring of stars. The ring in a ring galaxy is usually made up of many bright, young, blue stars. Ring galaxies don't form naturally, and are the result of a galaxy interacting with another galaxy or cloud of matter.

One ring to rule them all. Hoag's Object is a ring galaxy containing about 8 billion stars. Nobody knows for sure how it ended up shaped like this.

SCHWARZSCHILD RADIUS: The largest volume that a given mass could have and still be considered a black hole. For example, for the sun to become a black hole, all of the mass of the sun would have to be squished inside a sphere that has a diameter of less than two miles (3 km). The Schwarzschild radius for Earth is about a third of an inch (8.7 mm). The radius of an actual black hole can never be known, but the Schwarzschild radius for a black hole is equal to the black hole's event horizon.

SEYFERT GALAXY: A spiral galaxy with an unusually bright center. A Seyfert galaxy is like a dim quasar: In a quasar, the core is so bright it outshines the entire rest of the galaxy, but in a Seyfert galaxy the core isn't as bright, so the spiral galaxy is still visible. About one out of 10 galaxies in the universe is a Seyfert galaxy.

Galaxy light, galaxy bright! The supermassive black hole in the center of Seyfert galaxy NGC 6300 is about 300,000 times the mass of the sun.

SINGULARITY: A point in space where mass has been crushed into an infinitely small volume with infinite density. The center of a black hole is the most common example of a singularity. The Big Bang was a singularity that exploded.

STARS AND GALAXIES

SPIRAL GALAXY: A flat, circular galaxy with a bulge in the center and a pinwheel appearance. The Milky Way is a spiral galaxy. The bright central bulge of a spiral galaxy is usually made up of old stars, while the spiral arms are made of gas, dust, and young stars. New stars are always being formed in the flat circular disk of a spiral galaxy. Our sun lies about halfway out from the center of our galaxy on one of the spiral arms.

The Milky Way

You Are Here!

Out of this whirl! The Whirlpool Galaxy (NGC 5194) and its companion dwarf galaxy NGC 5195.

STAR: A large ball of plasma mostly made of hydrogen. A star is so dense in the center that hydrogen is fused into helium, releasing a massive amount of energy. A star's mass, color, lifespan, and temperature are all directly related: A more massive star will be brighter, hotter, bluer, and will burn out faster. Our sun is a type of star known as a yellow dwarf.

STAR CLUSTER: A group of stars all about the same age that are gravitationally bound together. There are two types of star clusters—*globular clusters* and *open clusters*. Globular clusters are small groups of hundreds or thousands of fairly old stars. Open clusters are looser groups of only a few hundred stars, which are usually fairly young. Globular clusters are usually found above and below the galactic disk, and open clusters are usually a part of the galactic disk.

M80 (NGC 6093)

Globular clusters

NGC 3572

Open clusters

STARBURST GALAXY: A galaxy that is producing stars very quickly. This normally happens when a galaxy interacts with another galaxy, and only occurs for a short time until the gas clouds in the galaxy that are available for making stars get used up.

STELLAR EVOLUTION: The changes that a star undergoes from the time it is born out of a cloud of dust and gas until it dies as a supernova or white dwarf. How long the process takes depends on how big the star is: Bigger stars have a shorter lifespans, some as short as only a million years. A star like our sun will live about 10 billion years. Some red dwarfs are almost as old as the universe and have enough fuel to last for trillions of years more. (See pp. 18–19.)

STELLAR WIND: A stream of high-energy, electrically charged particles (mostly protons and electrons) that flows outward from a star in all directions at speeds of more than a million miles per hour. A star's stellar wind is strongest near the end of its life when it has used up most of its fuel. The stellar wind from our sun is known as the solar wind.

NGC 6565

STARS AND GALAXIES

STARS AND GALAXIES

SUPERMASSIVE BLACK HOLE: A black hole that has a mass equal to that of millions or billions of stars. Supermassive black holes are usually found in the centers of galaxies, including the Milky Way. Scientists aren't sure how supermassive black holes are formed, but they think it might be by the collapse of gigantic clouds of dust and gas.

Hide and seek! The supermassive black hole in the center of galaxy NGC 1068 is partially hidden by thick clouds of gas and dust.

SUPERNOVA: When a large dying star explodes at the end of its lifetime, that event is called a supernova. The outer layers of the star are blown out into space, and the core of the star collapses down into either a neutron star or a black hole. The gases that are blown out from the exploding star form a nebula or glowing cloud in space known as a supernova remnant. A supernova is the biggest explosion ever seen in space.

I wanna see one! Well, you might get to. A galaxy like ours has about one supernova every 50 years, but we haven't seen one in the Milky Way for more than 300 years, so we're way overdue. If a star in our galaxy does go supernova, it might be bright enough to see during the day. The daytime star would last about a month, and the supernova would remain visible at night for 6 months to a year. After that you would need a telescope to see it.

SUPERNOVA REMNANT: The cloud of gas that was expelled from a star that has gone supernova. Most supernova remnants look a bit like giant soap bubbles in space, as they are hollow spheres of colorful glowing hot gas that expand outward from the core of the star. If a supernova remnant is large enough, it can become a nebula and new stars can form from the remains of the old one.

I'm not crabby! The Crab Nebula in the constellation Taurus is a supernova remnant from a star that exploded in 1054 A.D. It doesn't look anything like a crab, but William Parsons, the 3rd Earl of Rosse, who discovered it in 1840, drew a picture of it that looked a little like a crab, and the name stuck. You can't see the Crab Nebula with the naked eye, but on a clear night you can see it with good binoculars or a telescope. The star that exploded to form the Crab Nebula was too small to become a black hole, and its core collapsed into a pulsar (p. 48) in the center of the nebula.

The colors in the image indicate the different elements that were expelled during the explosion. Blue in the outer part of the nebula represents neutral oxygen, green is ionized sulfur, and red indicates ionized oxygen.

STARS AND GALAXIES

THERMAL RADIATION: Radiation coming from an object that tells astronomers how hot it is. Hotter objects give off bluer light, and colder objects give off redder light. Thermal radiation extends outside of the visible light region, so an object that is giving off lower-energy infrared light would be cooler than one that is giving off visible red light.

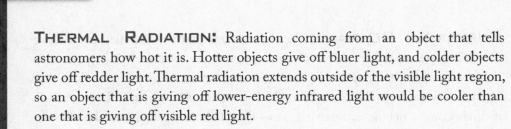

True or false? People glow in the dark.
        True! Warm-blooded animals, including humans, give off thermal radiation as infrared light. We can't see it, but some animals, including certain snakes, vampire bats, and bedbugs, can detect it. By using night vision goggles that detect infrared light and generate visible images, you can see people glow in the dark.

VARIABLE STAR: A star that seems to go through cycles of being brighter and dimmer over time. This might happen because the star naturally changes intensity with time or it might happen if a planet is passing in front of the star and blocking some of the star's light from reaching Earth.

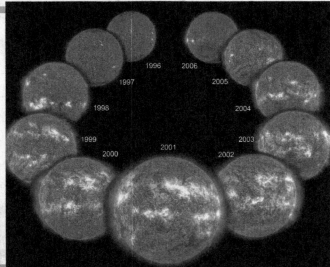

As constant as the sun? Our sun is a variable star that goes through 11-year cycles of brightness and dimness called *solar cycles*, but the variations in brightness are less than 1% and we don't notice it.

WHITE DWARF: The core of a small star that has recently died. It glows dimly because it is still hot from when the star was fusing, but no more fusion is happening. White dwarfs are mostly made of carbon and oxygen. White dwarfs are usually about the size of the Earth, but have a mass equal to that of the sun. Our sun will turn into a white dwarf when it dies. White dwarfs eventually cool off after billions of years and become black dwarfs.

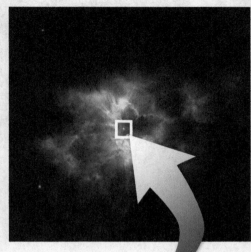

Like a Pearl. The planetary nebula, NGC 2440, contains one of the hottest white dwarf stars known. The portion of NGC 2440 shown spans about one light-year. The center of our sun will eventually become a white dwarf but not for another 5 billion years.

YELLOW DWARF: A star like our sun. Yellow dwarf stars are fairly ordinary in size and temperature, and are in the middle of their lifespan, fusing hydrogen into helium. When a yellow dwarf begins to run out of fuel it will expand and cool to become a red giant, and eventually collapse in on itself to become a white dwarf.

Jupiter

Proxima Centauri
Red Dwarf

The Sun
Yellow Dwarf

Sirius A
Main Sequence Star

THE SOLAR SYSTEM

YOU ARE HERE

Our solar system is a lot like a family, with eight or nine children orbiting a parent in the center. But if the solar system were a family, it would have to be a family of wacky misfits from some bizarre cartoon comedy.

In the center of it all is a big, fat, screaming parent, the sun. The sun is constantly erupting in violent outbursts, and its deadly solar wind continually washes over everything in the solar system. There's no getting away from this hot, angry parent because the sun's gravity keeps all of the kids grounded for life, trapped in their orbits and unable to escape.

Although all of the planet-children were formed at the same time as the sun and from the same cloud of gas and dust, no two planets are alike. Tiny Mercury, the baby of the family, is simultaneously roasting hot on one side and freezing cold on the other. Venus is a brutal pressure cooker that has destroyed every probe that ever landed there, like a stormy teenager screaming "Stay out of my room!" Easygoing Earth, meanwhile, is home to tropical beaches and winter ski resorts and rain forests and deserts—but cold, hard Mars, right next door, is a barren rock covered with rust. Things only get stranger from there, with the hulking big brother Jupiter, made of the same material as the sun, and glamorous Saturn, the beauty queen of the family, whose sparkling rings of ice and dust glitter against the darkness of space like a jeweled necklace. The ice giants Neptune and Uranus are the closest things to twins in our solar system family, except that unlike any of its brothers and sisters, Uranus orbits the sun while lying on its side. There may also be a long-lost ninth child in the family, a planet almost the size of Neptune but still undiscovered, keeping its distance from the rest of its kooky family in an orbit so far away we have never even seen it.

In addition to this crazy cast of oddball planets, the solar system is home to asteroids, meteoroids, and comets whose eccentric paths have them running through the house like of out of control cats and dogs, sometimes on a collision course with a planet or moon. Other small objects, composed mostly of ice and rock, quietly circle in the distant Kuiper belt like spectators pretending not to be part of the same family, but whether they like it or not, they're part of our solar system as well.

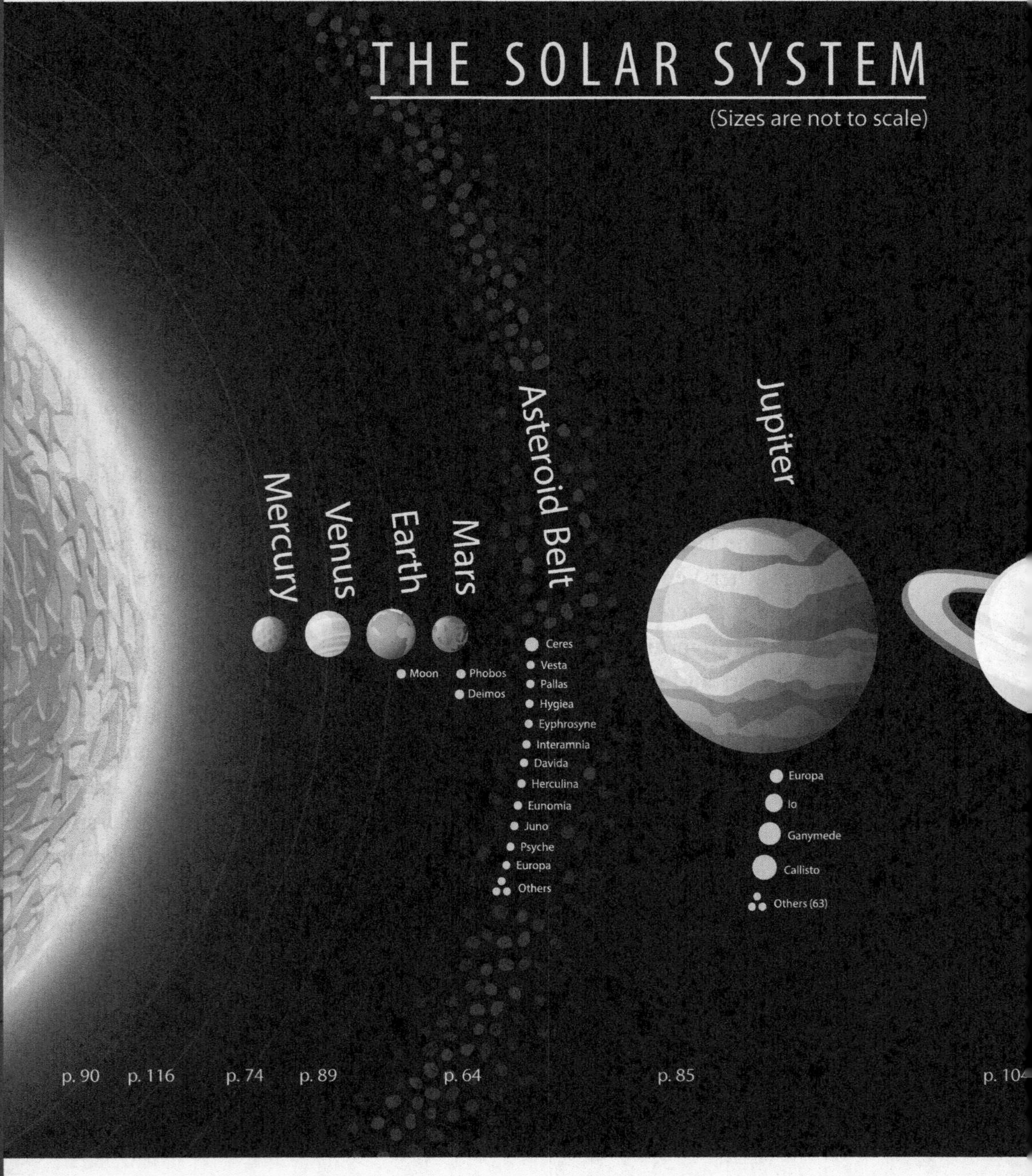

THE SOLAR SYSTEM
(Sizes are not to scale)

THE SOLAR SYSTEM

Jupiter

Asteroid Belt

Mercury

Venus

Earth

Mars

Moon

Phobos

Deimos

- Ceres
- Vesta
- Pallas
- Hygiea
- Eyphrosyne
- Interamnia
- Davida
- Herculina
- Eunomia
- Juno
- Psyche
- Europa
- Others

Europa

Io

Ganymede

Callisto

Others (63)

p. 90   p. 116   p. 74   p. 89   p. 64   p. 85   p. 104

This is our solar system. It's a crazy place with so much going on that the more we learn about the solar system, the more questions we have. These are some of the words planetary astronomers use when studying our solar system and the processes and interactions that occur within it.

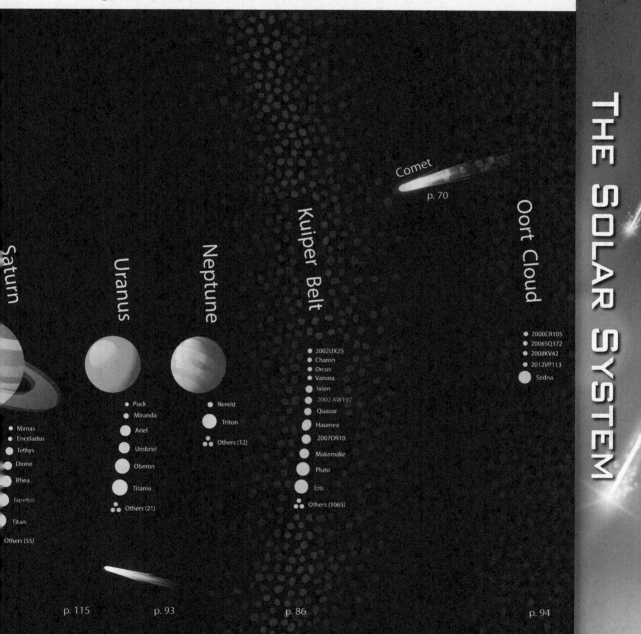

Comet
p. 70

Oort Cloud

Kuiper Belt

Neptune

Uranus

Saturn

- 2000CR105
- 2006SQ372
- 2008KV42
- 2012VP113
- Sedna

- 2002UX25
- Charon
- Orcus
- Varuna
- Ixion
- 2002 AW197
- Quaoar
- Haumea
- 2007OR10
- Makemake
- Pluto
- Eris
- Others (1065)

- Nereid
- Triton
- Others (12)

- Puck
- Miranda
- Ariel
- Umbriel
- Oberon
- Titania
- Others (21)

- Mimas
- Enceladus
- Tethys
- Dione
- Rhea
- Iapetus
- Titan
- Others (55)

p. 115   p. 93   p. 86   p. 94

THE SOLAR SYSTEM

61

THE SOLAR SYSTEM

ABLATION: When a meteor enters Earth's atmosphere, it heats up from friction with the air, and the outer surface of the meteor begins to burn up and tear away. This loss of material from the surface is called ablation. Ablation causes some meteors to erode away completely before they ever reach the Earth's surface.

AEROLITE: Aerolite is another word for a stony meteorite, which is a meteorite that is made up mostly of silicate rock. Silicate rock is the same kind of rock that makes up most of the Earth's crust, so it's hard to tell an aerolite from an ordinary Earth rock.

ALBEDO: Albedo is a measure of how well an object in space reflects light. Something that absorbs all light has an albedo of 0, and a perfect mirror that reflects all light would have an albedo of 1. The albedo of an object in the solar system can provide clues about its composition or texture.

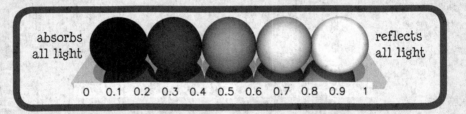

absorbs all light · 0 0.1 0.2 0.3 0.4 0.5 0.6 0.7 0.8 0.9 1 · reflects all light

ALBEDO FEATURE: A bright spot or dark spot that reflects light much better or worse than the surrounding area. The dwarf planet Ceres has many bright albedo features. Albedo features are often due to variations in the surface of a body, such as a flat plain that reflects light well or a rough surface that does not.

The dwarf planet Ceres

Albedo of the Planets

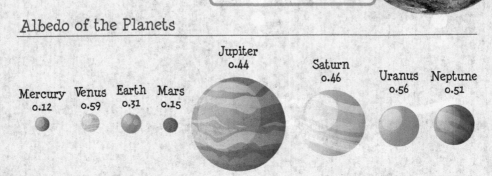

Mercury 0.12
Venus 0.59
Earth 0.31
Mars 0.15
Jupiter 0.44
Saturn 0.46
Uranus 0.56
Neptune 0.51

ANNULAR ECLIPSE: When the moon eclipses the sun at a point when the moon is farthest in its orbit from the Earth, the moon is not large enough in the sky to completely cover the sun. When this happens, a bright ring of sun remains visible around the circumference of the moon during the eclipse and the sun looks like a ring of fire in the sky. This kind of eclipse is known as an annular eclipse. *Annular* means "ring-shaped."

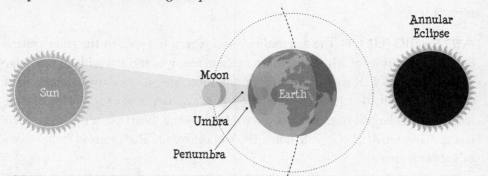

ANTIPODAL POINT: The antipodal point of a planet is the point on the exact opposite side of the planet from whatever you're talking about. The antipodal point of the North Pole is the South Pole.

> **That's a long, wet bus ride!** If you live in the continental United States, the antipodal point of your school is a spot in the Indian Ocean west of Australia.

APHELION: The point in a planet, asteroid, or comet's orbit around the sun where it is farthest from the sun. (See illustration on p. 97.)

APOGEE: The point in the orbit of the moon or other satellite around the Earth where it is farthest from the Earth. (See illustration on p. 97.)

APPARITION: This word has two meanings in astronomy, and neither of them is "ghost." Apparition can mean the moment when an object such as a comet first becomes visible after a period of time when it was not visible. Apparition can also refer to the range days that the object remains visible before it goes away again.

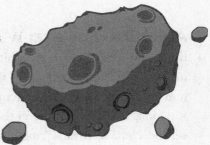

ASTEROID: A rocky object in space that's anywhere from about 30 feet to 620 miles (10 meters to 1,000 kilometers) across. Objects smaller than this are called *meteoroids*, and objects larger than this are *dwarf planets* or *planets*. Asteroids are also called *planetoids* or *minor planets*.

ASTEROID BELT: The asteroid belt is a region of space in the solar system between the orbits of Mars and Jupiter where many of the asteroids in our solar system are found. There are more than a million irregularly shaped asteroids in the asteroid belt, along with millions of smaller bodies down to the size of dust particles. The largest object in the asteroid belt is the dwarf planet Ceres, which has a diameter of about 598 miles (963 kilometers). The asteroid belt is also called *the main belt*.

Is the asteroid belt an exploded planet? No. If all of the material in the asteroid belt were gathered together it would only be about 4% of the size of the moon.

Asteroid, or aster-*void*? In science fiction movies, asteroid belts are usually chaotic regions of space filled with hurling boulders, but in real life the asteroid belt is mostly empty space. The average distance between main belt asteroids is about 5 million miles—more than 10 times farther apart than the Earth and the moon. When the Galileo space probe passed through the asteroid belt, the problem wasn't avoiding the asteroids, it was finding one close enough to study.

ASTEROID NUMBER: Every asteroid is assigned a number when its orbit is determined. The person who discovers a new asteroid can also name it if they choose to. There are currently more than 430,000 numbered asteroids in the solar system and about 250,000 more that are known, but not yet numbered. About 20,000 asteroids have names.

Name game! Which of these asteroid names is not real?

a. Monty Python
b. John, Paul, George, and Ringo
c. Mr. Spock
d. James Bond
e. Misterrogers

Answer: They are all real!

ASTRONOMICAL UNIT (AU): The average distance from the Earth to the sun, or about 93 million miles (150 million kilometers). This unit of length is used for measuring distances between objects within the solar system. For example, Neptune's orbit is an average 30.1 AU from the sun, so it is just more than 30 times farther from the sun than Earth is.

ATMOSPHERE: The layer of gases that surrounds a planet. A planet's atmosphere is held in place by the planet's gravity, which prevents the gases from escaping into space. The atmosphere becomes thinner and thinner the higher you go. There is no one point where the atmosphere "stops," but it is generally agreed that outer space begins 62 miles (100 km) above the Earth's surface. This point is known as the Kármán line.

Venus
Thick atmosphere containing 96% CO_2

Earth
Medium atmosphere containing 78% N_2, 21% O_2, only 0.039% CO_2

Mars
Thin atmosphere containing 96% CO_2

THE SOLAR SYSTEM

THE SOLAR SYSTEM

AU: See *Astronomical Unit*, p. 65.

AURORA: A colorful glow in the night sky that occurs high in the atmosphere above the polar regions of Earth. When the solar wind reaches Earth's upper atmosphere, it interacts with the Earth's magnetic field and releases energy in the form of light. The aurora at the North Pole is called the aurora borealis, or northern lights. The aurora at the South Pole is the aurora australis, or southern lights.

More auroras than our auroras. Say that three times fast! Other planets also have auroras at their magnetic poles. Jupiter and Saturn both have large auroras, and auroras have also been seen on Neptune and Uranus.

AXIS: An imaginary line that runs through the center of a rotating object like the axle of a wheel. The Earth's axis goes from the North Pole to the South Pole.

BINARY ASTEROID: Two asteroids that are orbiting one another. When the asteroids are close to the same size, they are sometimes called *binary companions* or *double asteroids*.

AXIAL TILT

ROTATION AXIS

EQUATOR

PERPENDICULAR TO ORBIT

BLUE MOON: Because the moon goes through a full cycle every 29 days, but most months have 30 or 31 days, sometimes there will be a full moon at the beginning of a month and a second full moon at the end of the same month. This second full moon in one month is called a *blue moon*. A blue moon can also be an extra moon that occurs in a particular season (four full moons in 3 months) or in a year (13 full moons in 12 months). A blue moon isn't really blue, and is just a regular full moon.

> **This name makes more sense.** The second new moon in a single month is called a black moon.

BODY: See *Celestial Body*, p. 68.

BOLIDE: An exceptionally bright meteor, which usually breaks up or even explodes from excessive heat as it travels through the atmosphere.

CALLISTO: Jupiter's second-largest moon, Callisto is essentially a planet-sized asteroid in orbit around Jupiter. Callisto is entirely composed of rock and ice just like an asteroid, but is almost the same size as Mercury. Unlike smaller asteroids, Callisto is massive enough that its gravity has pulled it into a sphere.

CANNIBAL CORONAL MASS EJECTION: An especially powerful coronal mass ejection (CME) that races outward from the sun and swallows up slower-moving CME's ahead of it. When a cannibal CME is directed toward Earth, it can disrupt satellites, navigation systems, and radio communications.

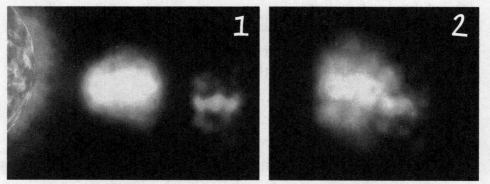

(1) A bright solar flare launches a coronal mass ejection followed by another. They meet in space and (2) merge into one.

THE SOLAR SYSTEM

THE SOLAR SYSTEM

CELESTIAL BODY: Any natural object outside of Earth's atmosphere.

CELESTIAL EQUATOR: If you take the Earth's equator and extend it out into space, that's called the celestial equator. The celestial equator is often used as a reference point when looking at the position of other celestial bodies. For example, the 2 days each year when the sun crosses the celestial equator are the equinoxes, and the 2 days when the sun is farthest from the celestial equator are the solstices.

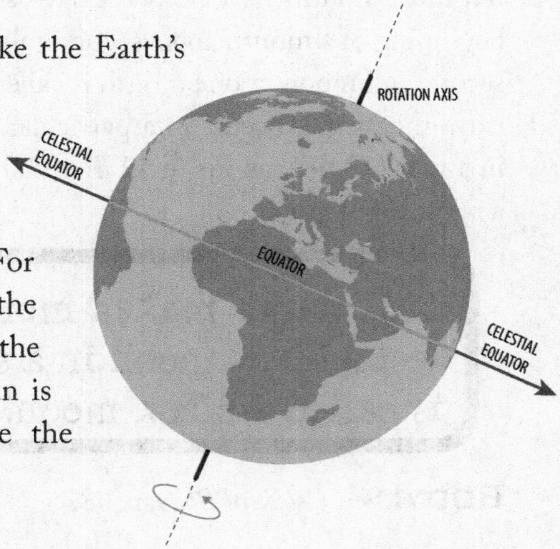

ROTATION AXIS

CELESTIAL EQUATOR

EQUATOR

CELESTIAL EQUATOR

CELESTIAL SPHERE: If you imagine that the Earth is in the center of a gigantic sphere, and the objects in the night sky are projected onto the inside of that sphere like a movie on a movie screen, then the sphere that all of the stars and planets are moving around on is called the celestial sphere. Early astronomers believed the celestial sphere was real, and it wasn't until the 1500s that they realized that there is no sphere and the stars are spread out at different distances from Earth.

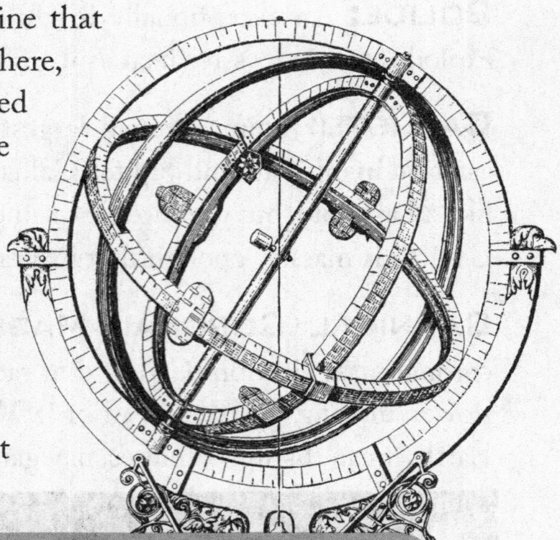

Not all who wander are lost. The stars and galaxies have fixed positions on the celestial sphere, but the sun and planets move around. The word *planet* comes from the Greek word for "wanderer."

CERES: A dwarf planet that is the largest object in the asteroid belt. By itself Ceres makes up a third of the total mass of all of the objects in the asteroid belt. Ceres has strong enough gravity to pull itself into a sphere, and is differentiated, which means it has a crust, mantle, and core, just as Earth does. There is ice on Ceres, but it has no atmosphere.

CHARON: The largest of Pluto's five moons and the one closest to it. Charon is about half the diameter of its host planet, which is unusually large for a moon.

Pluto
1,474 miles wide

Charon
754 miles wide

It must be love! Astronomers believe Charon and Pluto were minor planets that impacted one another and then began orbiting together.

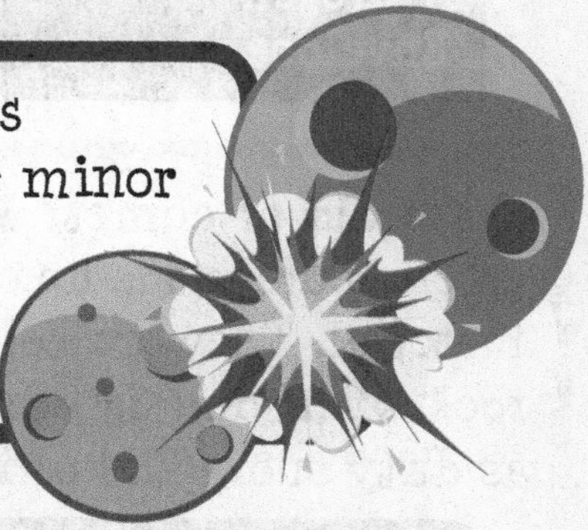

CIRCUMSTELLAR DISK: A ring or donut-shaped cloud of gas, dust, ice, and rocks (but not planets) in orbit around a star. In some cases, planets can form from the circumstellar disk, or a circumstellar disk may be left over after a planet is destroyed. The asteroid belt and Kuiper belt are two examples of circumstellar disks in our solar system.

COMA: A haze of dust and gas surrounding the nucleus of a comet.

COMET: A mass of icy rock that has a highly elliptical orbit around a star. When the comet is far away from the star, it looks a lot like a small asteroid—this is the comet's nucleus. As the comet gets closer to the star, it heats up and its surface begins to vaporize. This cloud of gas and dust coming off the nucleus shows up as the comet's coma and a tail, with the tail always pointed away from the star. As the comet moves away from the star again, the coma and tail die down and the nucleus continues its orbit until its next apparition.

COMET NUCLEUS: The central part of a comet made mostly of dust and ice, usually a few miles across.

Asteroid or comet? A comet's nucleus and an asteroid are made up of almost the exact same material. They are both composed mostly of rock with some ice, and are sometimes described as dirty snowballs or icy dirtballs.

Orbit in peace. Each trip past the sun burns away a little more of the comet's nucleus, until eventually everything that can be vaporized away is gone and only a large rock remains. This is called a *dead comet.*

CONJUNCTION: This word has two different meanings in astronomy. (1) A conjunction occurs when two objects in the night sky appear to come close together. For example, when the planets Venus and Jupiter move close together in the sky it is called a conjunction. (2) Any time another planet (or the moon) lies on a straight line with Earth and the sun.

CONSTELLATION: A pattern of stars as seen from Earth in the night sky that represents a picture of some kind. There are 88 constellations. The word "constellation" is sometimes used to describe not just the stars themselves but also the region of the night sky where those stars are located.

CORE: The central part of a planet, star, or galaxy. The composition of the core is different from other parts of the planet, star, or galaxy.

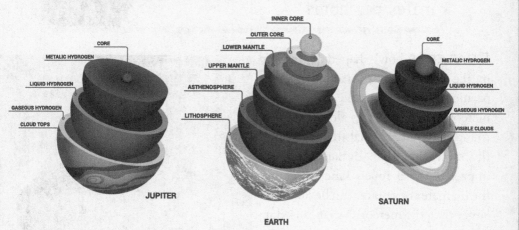

CORONA: The outermost layer of the sun's atmosphere. It is made up of billowing waves of hot plasma with a temperature of more than a million degrees, and extends millions of miles into space. Because the sun's surface is so bright, the corona is only visible during a solar eclipse. *Corona* comes from the Latin word meaning "crown."

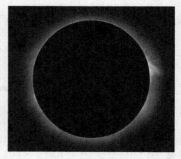

CORONAL MASS EJECTION (CME): A burst of hot plasma made up mostly of protons and electrons that shoots out of the sun's corona into space. When the sun is most active it can produce three CME's per day, and when it is least active it produces about one every 5 days. Sometimes CME's occur after solar flares, but they can occur even without solar flare activity.

Duck! A single coronal mass ejection can contain 10 billion tons of material and travel hundreds of millions of miles into space at a speed of a million miles per hour!

CRATER: A bowl-shaped depression in the surface of an asteroid, planet, or moon formed by the impact of a meteorite. Craters are almost always round no matter what the shape of the meteorite itself. Because meteors impact with so much kinetic energy, the diameter of a crater can be 50 times larger than the meteorite that caused it.

The Arizona Meteor Crater is 570 feet deep and 4,100 feet across and was created 50,000 years ago by an asteroid roughly 130 feet wide.

CRESCENT: A phase of the moon where less than half the surface is visible. This happens when the moon is going into or coming out of a new moon phase.

The men in the moons? If you lived on Saturn, it would be normal to see many moons in the sky. From largest to smallest in this photo, Titan, Rhea, and Mimas are all in the crescent phase.

CRUST: The thin outermost surface layer of a terrestrial planet or dwarf planet. The Earth's crust is about 20–30 miles thick on land and 6 miles thick beneath the oceans, compared to Earth's overall diameter of almost 8,000 miles.

> **A planet a day . . .** The Earth's crust is about as thick on the Earth as an apple's skin is on an apple.

DARK SIDE OF THE MOON: As the moon orbits around the Earth, the same side of the moon always faces Earth. The side that faces away from Earth was originally called the dark side of the moon, even though it receives just as much sunlight as the side that faces us. The side of the moon we cannot see is referred to now as the far side of the moon instead, and the dark side of the moon refers to the half of the moon that is facing away from the sun.

DEBRIS DISK: A ring of dust and rock the size of an entire solar system that is in orbit around a star. Some debris disks appear to be part of the formation of new solar systems, and are the next step after a protoplanetary disk. Other debris disks appear to be stable the way they are because planetesimals (asteroids and comets) continually smash into each other and prevent planets from forming.

DIRECT MOTION: Objects moving around the sun in the same direction as Earth's orbit are said to be moving in direct motion. When objects appear to move around the sun in the opposite direction of Earth's orbit, that is called *retrograde motion*.

Direct Motion   Direct Motion

Retrograde Motion (p. 102)

DOUBLE ASTEROID: See *Binary Asteroid*, p. 66.

THE SOLAR SYSTEM

THE SOLAR SYSTEM

DWARF PLANET: A celestial body orbiting the sun that is massive enough to be rounded into a ball by its own gravity, but which has not cleared the area around its orbit of planetesimals. Dwarf planets are larger than asteroids but smaller than planets. The largest dwarf planets in our solar system are Pluto and Eris near the outer edge of our solar system, and Ceres in the asteroid belt between Mars and Jupiter. The classification of dwarf planet was created in 2006 following the discovery of Eris.

Twinning? The dwarf planet Eris is known as Pluto's twin because of its similar size. Its discovery was a big reason why Pluto was demoted from planet status—a controversial decision.

EARTH: The third planet from the sun and the only planet in our solar system that is known to support life. Earth lies in the narrow celestial habitable zone around the sun where water exists on the surface of the planet in liquid form instead of only as ice or gaseous vapor. Earth is 93 million miles, or one astronomical unit (AU), away from the sun.

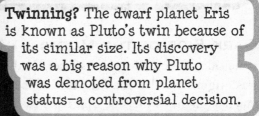

An "EPIC" View. This image of Earth was captured in 2015 by NASA's Earth Polychromatic Imaging Camera (EPIC). It was taken from a million miles away!

EARTHSHINE: When the moon is only partly lit by the sun, such as a crescent or gibbous moon, the dark portion isn't entirely dark: You can still sometimes make out details in the dark area because there is a faint light shining on it. This faint light is sunlight that is reflected off the Earth, and is called earthshine.

ECCENTRICITY: A measure of how much an orbit deviates from circular. All orbits are elliptical rather than circular, but some are more elliptical than others. A comet's orbit has much greater eccentricity than a planet's orbit.

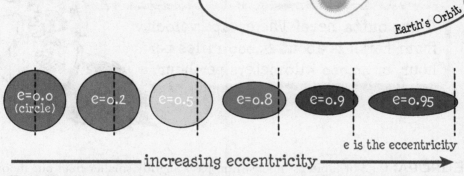

The dotted lines in each orbit shown above indicates the position of the sun. Earth's orbit is nearly circular, with an eccentricity of less than 0.02. Halley's Comet has an orbit with an eccentricity of 0.967.

ECLIPSE: When our view of one celestial body is blocked partially or totally by another celestial body that is moving in front of it. (See *Lunar Eclipse*, p. 87, and *Solar Eclipse*, p. 107.)

ECLIPTIC: If you could take the Earth's orbit around the sun and turn it into a flat surface, that flat surface would be the ecliptic. The 12 constellations of the Zodiac all lie on the ecliptic; the other 76 constellations are above or below the ecliptic.

ELLIPSE: An oval shape. Johannes Kepler discovered in the early 1600s that the orbits of the planets are not perfect circles as Copernicus said they were, but are actually slightly elliptical.

THE SOLAR SYSTEM

75

EQUINOX: There are two dates each year, usually on March 20 or 21 and on September 22 or 23, when the day and night are both 12 hours long. These dates are known as the equinoxes and are the first day of spring and the first day of fall. The vernal equinox occurs in the spring, and the autumnal equinox occurs in the fall.

ESCAPE VELOCITY: The minimum speed required for a flying object to overcome the gravitational pull of a planet or other body and escape into space.

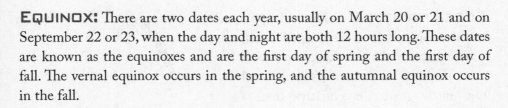

I am outta here! The escape velocity from Earth is about 25,000 miles per hour, or 40,000 kilometers per hour.

EUROPA: One of Jupiter's moons. Europa is slightly smaller than our moon and has a thin oxygen atmosphere, along with underground seas of salt water. Europa is currently considered to be the most likely place to find extraterrestrial life in our solar system.

EVENING STAR: Another name for the planet Venus when it is visible the evening sky. Venus looks like the brightest star in the sky because it reflects light from the sun. When Venus is out in the early morning, it is called the *morning star*.

Venus is brighter than all other planets or stars seen from Earth. The second brightest object seen here is Jupiter.

EXTRASOLAR: This word literally means beyond the sun, but usually refers to things that are outside our solar system.

EXTRATERRESTRIAL: A word used to describe anything that does not originate on Earth. Normally extraterrestrial is an adjective, but it is also used as a noun to mean an alien creature.

I know you are, but what am I? Terra is another name for Earth, and humans visiting other planets would be known as Earthlings or Terrans.

FAR SIDE OF THE MOON: The side of the moon that is always facing away from Earth. (See *Dark Side of the Moon*, p. 73.)

FIREBALL: A fireball is a meteor that is at least as bright as any of the planets in the night sky. Sometimes the word fireball is used synonymously with bolide, but bolides are exceptionally bright fireballs that break apart or explode before reaching Earth.

FIRST QUARTER: A phase of the moon that is half lit by the sun and half in shadow as it grows toward a full moon. In the Northern Hemisphere, the illuminated part of a first quarter moon is shaped like a capital D. A first quarter moon rises in the east around noon, is high overhead around 6 p.m., and sets in the west around midnight.

Phases of the Moon

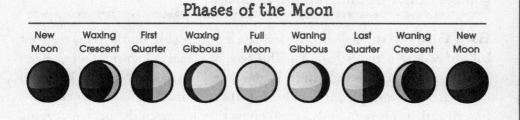

| New Moon | Waxing Crescent | First Quarter | Waxing Gibbous | Full Moon | Waning Gibbous | Last Quarter | Waning Crescent | New Moon |

THE SOLAR SYSTEM

FULL MOON: The phase of the moon when the sun lights up the full disk and the moon appears as a complete circle in the sky. At this point the sun and moon are on exact opposite sides of the Earth. A full moon rises at sunset, is overhead around midnight, and sets around sunrise.

GALILEAN MOONS: Jupiter's four largest moons, Io, Europa, Ganymede, and Callisto, which were discovered by Galileo, and also independently by a German astronomer named Simon Marius, in January 1610. Although they are known as the Galilean moons, they have the names Simon Marius chose for them.

GANYMEDE: Jupiter's largest moon. Ganymede's diameter is more than twice that of the planet Mercury. Ganymede is made up mostly of ice and rock, but has an iron core and an underground sea that may contain more water than all of Earth's oceans put together.

How do we know? How can we possibly know there's an underground ocean on Ganymede? The Hubble Space Telescope showed us that Ganymede has auroras (p. 66) that are a lot like the aurora borealis on Earth. Jupiter's powerful magnetic field causes these auroras to move on Ganymede, but they don't move as much as the calculations say they should. This means something inside of Ganymede is acting to oppose Jupiter's magnetic field, and the best explanation for this is a huge underground saltwater ocean.

GAS GIANT: Not all planets are solid rocky spheres like Earth. Many are giant balls of hydrogen and helium gas. This type of planet is known as a gas giant. Jupiter and Saturn are gas giants. In the past, Uranus and Neptune have also been referred to as gas giants, but because they are made up of heavier elements (mostly carbon, nitrogen, and oxygen) rather than hydrogen and helium, they are more often referred to as ice giants instead.

GEOCENTRIC: An adjective that means Earth is in the center. Based on their observations of the night sky, the earliest astronomers believed Earth was in the center of the universe and that the sun, the stars, and the planets all revolved around the Earth. They thought the Earth itself did not move.

GEOSYNCHRONOUS ORBIT: When a satellite is put into orbit, its altitude and speed can be matched to the rotation of the Earth so that the satellite returns to the same spot above the Earth at the same time each day. This is known as a geosynchronous orbit.

GEOSYNCHRONOUS ORBIT

EQUATOR

GEOSTATIONARY ORBIT

GIBBOUS: The phase of the moon when the moon is more than half full, but less than completely full.

GREAT RED SPOT: A massive, swirling storm in Jupiter's upper atmosphere that was first seen in the year 1665. At its largest recorded size, the storm was an oval almost as wide as three planet Earths, but since at least the late 1800s it has been shrinking and becoming more circular, and is now about 1.5 times as wide as the Earth. The Great Red Spot has winds that blow more than 400 miles per hour. The Great Red Spot is also changing from red to orange. Astronomers don't know why the storm appears red or why it is changing color as it shrinks.

Nearly 12,400 miles across

Great Red Not?

Although the Great Red Spot has been shrinking for more than a century, astronomers don't think it will ever go away completely. Most likely the storm will stabilize at a smaller size and then stop shrinking.

THE SOLAR SYSTEM

HALLEY'S COMET: A comet that is visible from Earth every 75 or 76 years. It passed by the Earth in 1986, and will return in the summer of 2061. The same comet had been seen on each return since at least 240 B.C., but it wasn't until 1705 that Edmond Halley realized all those appearances were the same comet over and over again.

HELIOCENTRIC: An adjective that means the sun is in the center. Copernicus was the first astronomer since ancient times to realize that the Earth orbits the sun instead of the other way around. That changed our understanding of the solar system from a geocentric one in which Earth was in the center to a heliocentric one that correctly put the sun in the center.

HELIOPAUSE: The sun gives off a constant stream of charged particles known as the solar wind, and the farther you get from the sun the weaker this flow of particles becomes. The heliopause is the point where it's so weak it gets stopped by the stellar winds from other stars. This is one way to define the edge of our solar system, and happens at 121 AU from the sun. (121 AU from the sun falls beyond the Kuiper belt, but well before the Oort Cloud begins.)

See ya, system! On August 25, 2012, the space probe Voyager 1, launched in 1977, crossed the heliopause and left our solar system for interstellar space. Voyager 2 should cross the heliopause in 2016. Both probes are expected to continue sending data until about 2025.

HELIOSPHERE: The spherical region inside the boundary of the heliopause. This is the region of space that is affected by the solar wind, and is effectively the entire volume of our solar system.

ICE: In everyday life, ice just means frozen water, but in astronomy, it can mean frozen water, frozen ammonia, or frozen methane. These are also sometimes called frozen gases. All of these are plentiful in the outer solar system, especially on Uranus and Neptune.

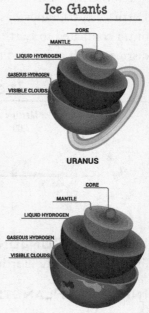

Ice Giants

CORE
MANTLE
LIQUID HYDROGEN
GASEOUS HYDROGEN
VISIBLE CLOUDS

URANUS

ICE GIANT: A giant planet that is made up of elements that are heavier than hydrogen and helium. Neptune and Uranus are ice giants, and are mostly made up of compounds that contain carbon, nitrogen, and oxygen, compared with the gas giants Jupiter and Saturn, which are almost entirely hydrogen and helium. Ice giants are still gassy on the surface, but have frozen gases such as methane, ammonia, and water ice in their mantles.

CORE
MANTLE
LIQUID HYDROGEN
GASEOUS HYDROGEN
VISIBLE CLOUDS

NEPTUNE

IMPACT: A collision between two planetary bodies. If one of the bodies is much smaller than the other, such as a meteorite impacting with Earth, it might leave a crater, which is also called an *impact crater*. Impacts between bodies of roughly equal size can shatter one or both bodies.

BAM!

A planetary impact such as this between the Earth and another body is believed to have formed the moon.

INCLINATION: The orbits of the planets in our solar system do not all lie in the same flat plane. Most of them are pretty close, but each one is a little different. Inclination is the angle of how tilted each planet's orbit is compared to Earth's orbit. Uranus has the lowest orbital inclination, at less than one degree of tilt compared to Earth's orbit. Mercury has the highest orbital inclination at 7 degrees of tilt compared to Earth's orbit.

Inclination of the Planets

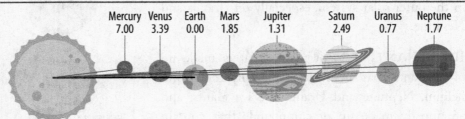

Mercury	Venus	Earth	Mars	Jupiter	Saturn	Uranus	Neptune
7.00	3.39	0.00	1.85	1.31	2.49	0.77	1.77

INFERIOR CONJUNCTION: When Mercury or Venus lies on a straight line in between the Earth and the sun.

INFERIOR PLANET: A planet whose orbit lies between Earth's orbit and the sun. Mercury and Venus are the only two inferior planets in our solar system. Sometimes the term inferior planet is used to mean any planet whose orbit is smaller than the orbit of the planet you're talking about: For example, Earth is an inferior planet to Mars, and all of the other planets are inferior to Neptune. (See *Superior Planet*, p. 111.)

INNER PLANET: Any of the planets in our solar system that are closer to the sun than the asteroid belt. These are the small rocky planets Mercury, Venus, Earth, and Mars.

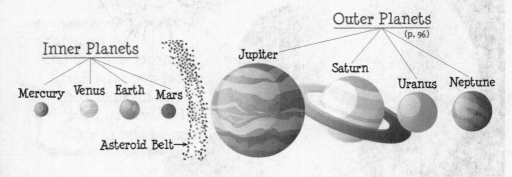

Inner Planets

Mercury Venus Earth Mars

Asteroid Belt→

Outer Planets
(p. 96)

Jupiter Saturn Uranus Neptune

The Solar System

INTERPLANETARY: The space in between the planets, or something that involves more than one planet such as an interplanetary space mission.

Highway to the cosmos. This space "freeway," envisioned by a NASA engineer, was designed for NASA's Genesis mission and finds paths through gravity fields for spacecraft to travel. It can be used to calculate the amount of fuel needed for interplanetary space missions.

INTERPLANETARY MAGNETIC FIELD: A magnetic field that stretches out from the sun throughout our solar system. The interplanetary magnetic field is created by the solar wind.

INTERPLANETARY MATTER: Traces of dust, gas, and other debris that are found between the planets in the solar system.

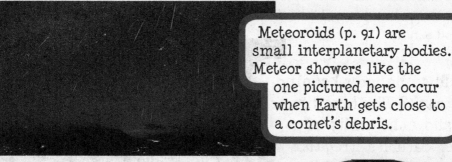

Meteoroids (p. 91) are small interplanetary bodies. Meteor showers like the one pictured here occur when Earth gets close to a comet's debris.

IO: One of Jupiter's four large moons. Io is caught in a gravitational tug of war between Jupiter and its other large moons, resulting in a surface on Io that is peppered with active volcanoes.

Hot and cold! Io's average surface temperature is -200°F, but it is pockmarked with volcanoes that are as hot as 3000°F.

THE SOLAR SYSTEM

83

IONIZED GAS: See *Plasma*, p. 47.

IRON METEORITE: A meteorite that is made up mostly of iron mixed with nickel. Less than 1 in 20 meteorites is an iron meteorite. Iron meteorites are pieces of the cores from shattered planetesimals.

This iron meteorite, called Lebanon, was found on Mars by NASA's Curiosity rover in 2014.

IRREGULAR MOON: An irregular moon is a moon that orbits its planet in an eccentric and inclined orbit. Irregular moons are believed to have been passing rocks that were captured by the planet's gravity. Our solar system has 113 irregular moons orbiting the four outer planets, most of them around Jupiter and Saturn.

Is somebody keeping track? The blue lines show the orbits of Saturn's irregular moons. The red oval in the center shows the orbit of Titan, a regular moon, for comparison.

JOVIAN PLANET: Any of the four large, outer, gaseous planets: Jupiter, Saturn, Uranus, and Neptune. The term is sometimes also used to describe a gas giant exoplanet that is similar in size and composition to Jupiter.

JUPITER: The largest planet in our solar system, Jupiter is twice as massive as all of the other planets combined and is named after the king of all the Roman gods. Jupiter is a gas giant made up of the same materials as the sun: about 89% hydrogen and 11% helium, with trace amounts of other elements. Jupiter has four large moons and 63 smaller ones, along with a faint ring system. Jupiter's orbit is more than five times farther from the sun than Earth is. One year on Jupiter is about 12 Earth years.

True or false?
Jupiter is a star that failed to ignite.
False! Jupiter is made up of the same elements as our sun, but it would have to be about 80 times more massive than it is before it could start fusing hydrogen and become a star.

KÁRMÁN LINE: A distance 62 miles (100 km) above the Earth where it is generally agreed that outer space begins.

Outer space is 62 miles away. On land, that's only about an hour's drive.

THE SOLAR SYSTEM

85

KEPLER'S LAWS OF PLANETARY MOTION: In the early 1600s, German astronomer Johannes Kepler came up with three laws describing the motion of planets in orbit around a sun: (1) Planets move in elliptical (oval-shaped) orbits around the sun, with the sun at one focus of the ellipse. (2) Planets that are closer to the sun move faster in their orbits and planets that are farther away move slower. (3) The farther away from the sun a planet's orbit is, the longer it will take that planet to circle the sun.

Life in the fast lane! Mercury flies through space at more than 100,000 mph. Neptune orbits at about 12,000 mph. One year on Mercury is only 88 days long, and a year on Neptune is almost 165 years long.

KIRKWOOD GAPS: Six regions in the main asteroid belt where almost no asteroids can be found. This is due to the fact that Jupiter's gravity changes the orbit of any object that enters these regions and either moves them elsewhere in the belt or ejects them from the asteroid belt altogether.

KUIPER BELT: A broad region in our outer solar system beyond the orbit of Neptune that is home to a vast array of small bodies made of icy rock, known as Kuiper belt objects (KBOs). The Kuiper belt stretches from about 30 AU from the sun to 50 AU, making it 20 times wider than the asteroid belt. It contains up to 200 times as much material as the asteroid belt, including the dwarf planets Pluto and Eris. Many of the short-period comets in our solar system are believed to be KBO's that were perturbed out of the Kuiper belt into highly eccentric orbits around the sun.

What is that? Strangely-shaped Haumea, named for the Hawaiian goddess of fertility, is a KBO and dwarf planet that is one of the fastest rotating large objects in the solar system.

LAST QUARTER: See *Third Quarter*, p. 112.

LATITUDE: A measure of how far north or south of the equator an object in the night sky is. Latitude ranges from 0 to 90 degrees. If the latitude of an object is 0 degrees, that means the object is directly above the equator. If an object's latitude is 90 degrees north it is above the North Pole, and if it is 90 degrees south it is above the South Pole.

LIMB: The outer edge of a planet or other celestial body in space. When you see the rounded edge of the moon at night, that is the limb of the moon.

LONG-PERIOD COMET: A comet that takes more than 200 years between appearances. Long-period comets have highly eccentric orbits, and most of them only pass through the inner solar system once. Hale–Bopp is an example of a long-period comet.

Comet Hale-Bopp is also called the Great Comet of 1997.

LUNA: The Latin name for our moon.

LUNAR: Having to do with the moon.

LUNAR CORONA: Sometimes the moon appears to have a faint ring of light surrounding it at night. This halo of light is caused by moonlight being diffracted by the Earth's atmosphere and is called a lunar corona.

LUNAR ECLIPSE: A darkening of the moon caused when Earth passes between the sun and the moon and Earth's shadow falls over the moon. This can only happen during a full moon.

LUNAR MONTH: The amount of time that passes between successive full moons or successive new moons. A lunar month is 29 days 12 hours and 44 minutes. This is how long it takes the moon to make one complete orbit around the Earth. A lunar month is also called a *synodic month* or a *lunation*.

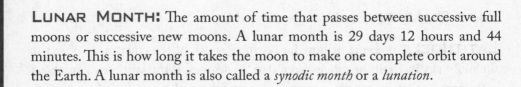

Must be a full moon tonight! Centuries ago people thought odd behavior was caused by the moon, and insane people were said to be *moonstruck*. The modern word *lunatic* also implies that the moon is to blame.

MAGNETIC FIELD: Many planets including Earth have iron cores that act as giant magnets. These magnets create a region of space around the planet called a magnetic field. The Earth's magnetic field helps protect the Earth from cosmic rays by steering them around the planet.

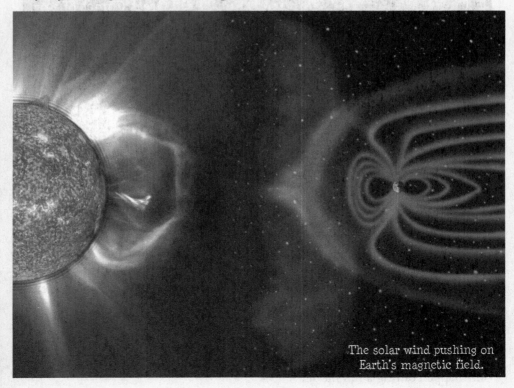

The solar wind pushing on Earth's magnetic field.

MAGNETIC POLE: The opposite ends of a magnet where the magnetic forces are strongest are known as the magnetic poles. Earth's magnetic poles are a few hundred miles from its geographic North and South Poles.

Upsy-daisy! The Earth's magnetic North and South Poles switch places about once every 450,000 years on average. It has been 780,000 years since the last geomagnetic reversal, and some scientists believe the next one could begin during our lifetimes.

MAIN BELT: Another name for the asteroid belt that lies between the orbits of Mars and Jupiter. Asteroids that orbit here are referred to as *main belt asteroids*.

MAJOR PLANET: A regular planet, as opposed to a dwarf planet or a minor planet. Our solar system has eight major planets.

MARE: A dark, flat region on the surface of the moon. The word *mare* is Latin for "sea," because early astronomers thought these dark regions on the moon were actual seas. The Sea of Tranquility where Apollo 11 landed is a mare.

MARS: Also known as the red planet, Mars is the first planet after Earth as you move away from the sun. The reddish color of Mars is due to high levels of iron oxide (rust) in its soil. Mars has mountains, valleys, volcanoes, and polar ice caps, and a thin atmosphere made up almost entirely of carbon dioxide. There is evidence that Mars once had surface water and may even have supported microscopic forms of life, but this has not yet been proven.

Night fright! Mars was the Roman god of war, known to the Greeks as Ares. Mars's two moons, Phobos and Deimos, are named after the twin sons of Ares in Greek mythology. Their names mean "fear" and "terror."

THE SOLAR SYSTEM

THE SOLAR SYSTEM

MERCURY: the smallest planet in our solar system and the one closest to the sun, Mercury has a cratered surface that looks like the moon. Daytime temperatures on Mercury can reach as high as 800°F (425°C), with nighttime temperatures as low as -280°F (-175°C).

METEOR: When a meteoroid enters Earth's atmosphere it heats up and glows and appears as a bright streak of light in the sky. This is called a meteor. Meteors are also called *shooting stars*. A very large and bright meteor is called a *fireball*, and a fireball that gets so hot that it explodes is called a *bolide*.

METEOR SHOWER: A meteor shower occurs when a large number of meteors enter the Earth's atmosphere from the same direction in space over a period of a few hours. Most meteor showers take place when the Earth passes through a debris field of ice and rock left behind by a comet. The Perseid meteor shower, which is visible every August in the Northern Hemisphere, produces up to 100 meteors per hour and is made up of pieces from Comet Swift–Tuttle.

METEORITE: When a meteor survives its journey through the atmosphere and reaches the Earth's surface, it is called a meteorite. Meteorites look like rocks or chunks of metal, and normally range in size from grains of sand to small rocks.

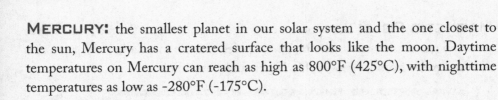

How to tell a meteorite from an ordinary rock:

> A freshly-fallen meteorite will have a dark "skin" on the surface but be lighter-colored inside.
> Meteorites often have shiny flecks of iron and nickel, and magnets will stick to them.
> Some meteorites look like they are made up of thousands of tiny round rocks all mashed together.
> Iron meteorites are surprisingly heavy for their size and might look like metal slag.
> Some meteorites look so much like Earth rocks that you can't tell the difference without doing a laboratory analysis.

METEOROID: Any small rock or particle of debris in outer space that is smaller than an asteroid. Meteoroids range in size from dust particles up to about 30 feet (10 meters) across.

Meteoroid

Meteor

Meteor

-ors, -oids, and -ites!
A meteoroid becomes a meteor when it enters Earth's atmosphere, and if it reaches the ground it becomes a meteorite.

Earth's Atmosphere

MICROGRAVITY: When you get far enough away from any large bodies in outer space gravity drops off to such a low level you don't feel it anymore, but it never fully goes away. These extremely low levels of gravity are called microgravity.

MICROMETEORITES: A meteorite that is less than 2 millimeters (1/12 inch) in diameter. These are too small to be found on land, and are usually found by melting polar ice and filtering it for tiny dust grains.

MICROMETEOROID: Another word for space dust. Most of the interplanetary solid material that is scattered throughout our solar system is in the form of micrometeoroids.

MIMAS: One of Saturn's 53 named moons, Mimas is an unremarkable, asteroid-sized moon that is noteworthy two reasons: (1) With a diameter of only 246 miles, Mimas is the smallest object in the solar system that is rounded by its own gravity, and (2) it has a particularly large crater that makes Mimas resemble the Death Star from *Star Wars*.

Herschel Crater is 80 miles wide

THE SOLAR SYSTEM

THE SOLAR SYSTEM

MINOR PLANET: Another word for an *asteroid*.

MOON: Also called a *natural satellite*, a moon is any rocky object orbiting a planet, dwarf planet, or asteroid. There are 173 known moons orbiting six planets in the solar system. Earth has one moon, Mars has two, and the rest orbit the outer giants. Many of the moons orbiting the gas giants are very small. Pluto also has moons, and some asteroids have moons as well. Mercury and Venus do not have moons.

Planet	# of Moons	Planet	# of Moons
Mercury	0	Jupiter	67
Venus	0	Saturn	62
Earth	1	Uranus	27
Mars	2	Neptune	14

MOON (EARTH'S MOON): Earth's moon is unusually large compared to the size of its planet. The moon is believed to be a large chunk of Earth's crust and mantle that was shattered off when Earth smashed into a Mars-sized object during the early formation of the solar system. Gravity caused the pieces from that collision to gather together and form a round moon.

MORNING STAR: This is not actually a star, but is another name for the planet Venus when it is visible the early morning sky. Venus looks like the brightest star in the sky because it reflects light from the sun. When Venus is out in the evening, it is called the *evening star*.

MULTIPLE STAR SYSTEM: See *Binary Star*, p. 23.

NEPTUNE: The farthest known planet in our solar system, Neptune is an ice giant made up mostly of methane, ammonia, and water that give it a blue color. Neptune has a diameter nearly four times the size of Earth. Neptune has a faint ring system and 14 moons, although Neptune's largest moon, Triton, makes up 99.7% of the mass of all of Neptune's moons, and the other 13 moons add up to only 0.3% of the total. Neptune has made only one orbit around the sun since its discovery in 1846.

> **Splash party!** Neptune was the Roman god of the sea, and Neptune's 14 moons are named after Neptune's children and minor sea gods and goddesses.

NEW MOON: The phase of the moon in which the moon is not visible in the night sky because the moon is out during the day with its lit side facing the sun. A new moon rises at dawn, is directly overhead around noon, and sets around sunset. A solar eclipse can only happen during a new moon.

NORTH STAR: The star that is straight up from the Earth's North Pole is called the North Star. The name of this particular star is Polaris. It is the last star in the handle of the Little Dipper (Ursa Minor).

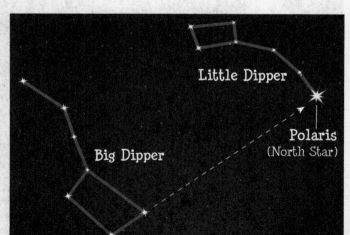

Little Dipper

Big Dipper

Polaris
(North Star)

THE SOLAR SYSTEM

NUCLEUS: The central core of an atom, comet, or galaxy. The nucleus of an atom is made up of protons and neutrons and contains nearly all of the mass of the atom. The nucleus of a comet is an icy rock that becomes the center of the comet's head (or coma) when it approaches a star. The nucleus of a galaxy is a dense region of stars and may also contain a black hole.

Nucleus of an atom

Nucleus of a comet

Nucleus of a galaxy

OBLATE SPHEROID: Most planets are not perfectly round, they are more like slightly squashed spheres that are a little shorter from top to bottom and a little wider around the middle. This kind of squashed spherical shape is called an oblate spheroid.

OORT CLOUD: A gigantic spherical cloud of icy planetesimals that surrounds our solar system. The Oort cloud lies a thousand times farther from the sun than the Kuiper belt, and stretches halfway to Proxima Centauri, the next nearest star to our sun. The Oort cloud is home to billions of comets. Even though objects in the Oort cloud are bound to the sun by gravity, the Oort cloud is considered to be outside of our solar system because it is well beyond the heliopause, or the point where the solar wind dies down to nothing.

Oort Cloud

Oort Cloud

No place like home. The comet in this diagram, C/2014 S3 (PANSTARRS), likely formed near the Earth but spent billions of years in the Oort cloud. It's currently headed back toward Earth, according to researchers, but it has a long way to travel! It's believed it could provide clues about the formation of the solar system.

OPPOSITION: When a planet such as Mars is at a place in its orbit that the sun, Earth, and the planet all lie on a straight line with the Earth in the center, the planet is said to be in opposition. Only planets whose orbits are farther from the sun than Earth's can be in opposition. Planets appear brightest in the night sky when they are in opposition. If we could see phases of Mars the way we can see phases of the moon, opposition would be a "full Mars."

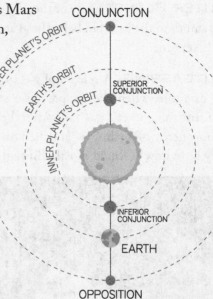

CONJUNCTION

OUTER PLANET'S ORBIT

EARTH'S ORBIT

INNER PLANET'S ORBIT

SUPERIOR CONJUNCTION

INFERIOR CONJUNCTION

EARTH

OPPOSITION

ORBIT: The elliptical path that an object follows as it goes around a bigger object, such as a moon around a planet or a planet around a star.

ORBITAL PERIOD: The length of time it takes for one body to orbit another. Earth's orbital period around the sun is one year. The moon's orbital period around Earth is about 29 days, or one lunar month. The precise amount of time in Earth days it takes for each planet to complete its orbit can be seen below.

Planet	# of Days
Mercury	88 days (0.2 years)
Venus	225 days (0.6 years)
Earth	365 days (1 year)
Mars	687 days (2 years)

Planet	# of Days
Jupiter	4,333 days (12 years)
Saturn	10,756 days (30 years)
Uranus	30,687 days (84 years)
Neptune	60,190 days (165 years)

THE SOLAR SYSTEM

OUTER PLANET: Any of the planets in our solar system that is farther from the sun than the asteroid belt. These are the giant planets Jupiter, Saturn, Uranus, and Neptune.

OUTGASSING: A release of gas from rocky body. This happens with comets, for example, when they approach a star and the frozen ice sublimates to gas to form the comet's gas tail. After Venus, Earth, and Mars lost their primary atmospheres of hydrogen and helium, their secondary atmospheres (the ones they have now) formed mostly through outgassing.

This image illustrates water outgassing from the dwarf planet Ceres, a discovery made in 2014.

PENUMBRA: The lighter part of a shadow that is found along the shadow's edge. The darker center of the shadow is called the *umbra*.

PENUMBRAL ECLIPSE: When the moon passes into the outer edge of Earth's shadow, causing a slight darkening in the moon's appearance.

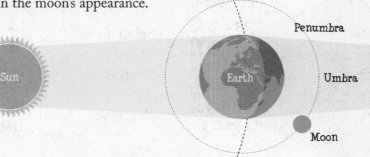

PERI-: A number of words all begin with the prefix *peri-*, and they all refer to when an orbiting body is at its closest point to the object it is orbiting. The opposites of these, when the orbiting object is at its farthest point from its host, uses a prefix *ap-* or *apo-* (apoapsis, apastron, apogee, and aphelion).

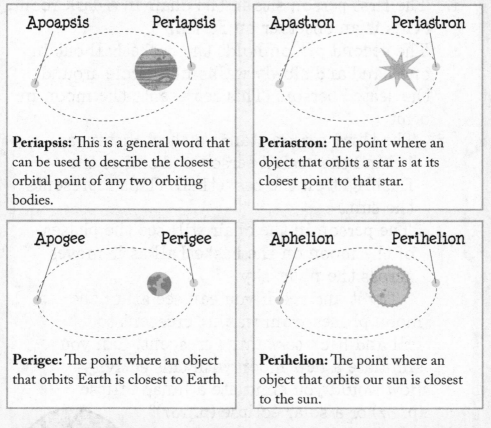

Periapsis: This is a general word that can be used to describe the closest orbital point of any two orbiting bodies.

Periastron: The point where an object that orbits a star is at its closest point to that star.

Perigee: The point where an object that orbits Earth is closest to Earth.

Perihelion: The point where an object that orbits our sun is closest to the sun.

PERIODIC COMET: A comet that has been seen to orbit the sun more than once. Periodic comets typically have orbital periods that are less than 200 years. The most famous periodic comet is Halley's Comet, whose orbital period is about 76 years.

PERTURBATION: A disturbance in the orbit of one celestial object caused by the gravitational pull of another celestial object.

PHASE: The apparent change in the shape of the moon as it moves around the Earth. The sun always lights up half of the moon, and the changes in phase are due to how much of that sunlit side of the moon is visible from Earth.

Try this!

You'll need three people, one chair, a basketball, a flashlight, and a dark room.

1. The first person sits in the chair in a dark room. (This is an observer on Earth.)
2. The second person holds the basketball out in one hand and slowly walks in a circle around the seated person. (This represents the moon in orbit.)
3. The third person stands a short distance behind the seated person and shines the flashlight on the basketball. (This represents the sun.)
4. The person in the chair will see the phases of the moon on the basketball as it moves across the night sky.

Try it and see if you can see all of the moon phases from waxing crescent to full and back to waning crescent. Can you simulate a new moon with this activity? How would you simulate a lunar eclipse (p. 87) or a solar eclipse (p. 107)?

PHOTOSPHERE: The visible surface layer of the sun. Stars don't have solid surfaces, and what we call the surface of the sun is really a swirling mass of plasma at about 10,000°F.

PLANET: In 2006, the International Astronomical Union redefined planet to be a body in space that orbits a star, is massive enough to have pulled itself into a sphere, and has cleared the neighborhood around its orbit of planetisemals. Because Pluto's orbit is littered with smaller objects, it no longer qualified as a planet and became classified as a dwarf planet.

PLANETARY-MASS OBJECT: A planet-sized object that drifts through outer space and does not orbit a star. A planetary-mass object is sometimes called a *planemo* for short. Most planetary-mass objects are gas giants that may have once belonged to solar systems until they were ejected from their orbits by gravitational interactions with some other massive object. These wandering planets are also known as rogue planets or nomad planets.

PLANETESIMAL: Chunks of rock and ice that range in size anywhere from 1 kilometer (0.6 miles) to 10 kilometers (6 miles) wide. Asteroids and comets are two examples of planetesimals.

PLANET NINE: Calculations on the orbits of objects in the Kuiper belt suggest that there is a large object orbiting our sun 75 times more distant than Pluto. This object has been called Planet Nine and is estimated to be two to four times the size of Earth but weigh 10 times as much as Earth does. Calculations indicate that Planet Nine would orbit the sun only once every 20,000 years. As of early 2016 Planet Nine has not been directly seen, and only mathematical evidence exists to suggest it is real.

THE SOLAR SYSTEM

It's happened before, you know! Neptune was also predicted mathematically before it was ever seen, and was found to be almost exactly where the mathematics said it would be.

THE SOLAR SYSTEM

PLUTO: A dwarf planet beyond Neptune's orbit. Pluto was considered to be a planet from 1930 to 2006, when new discoveries revealed similar-sized objects in the same area of space. Pluto's internal composition is ice and rock, similar to an asteroid or comet, making Pluto more like a very large asteroid than a planet.

The girl who named a planet. The name Pluto was suggested by 11-year-old Venetia Burney from England.

PRECESSION: In addition to orbiting the sun and rotating on its axis, the Earth has a third circular motion, called precession. In the same way that a spinning top begins to wobble before it falls down, the Earth wobbles very slowly as it rotates on its axis. This wobbling is called precession. It takes the Earth about 26,000 years to complete one full wobble (one period of precession). Because of precession, Earth's North and South Poles are always slowly changing the directions they point to in space.

Pick a star, any star! The North Star changes due to Earth's precession. Polaris is currently the North Star, but in 3000 B.C. the North Pole pointed toward a star named Thuban in the constellation Draco. In 13,000 years, the North Pole will point toward a star named Vega. Another 13,000 years after that, it will be back to pointing at Polaris.

PRIMARY ATMOSPHERE: A primary atmosphere is an atmosphere around a planet that was formed directly from the protoplanetary disk at the same time the planet itself formed. Because the protoplanetary disk was a dense mass of mostly hydrogen and helium, that's what a primary atmosphere is made of. The atmospheres of Jupiter and Saturn are primary atmospheres. (See *Secondary Atmosphere*, p. 105.)

PROMINENCE: An explosion of ionized gas that erupts from the sun's lower atmosphere (the chromosphere), and can extend more than 100,000 miles into space. That's about 12 times the diameter of Earth.

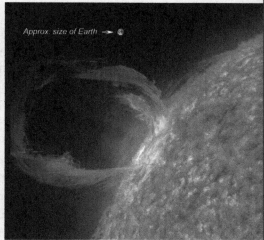

Approx. size of Earth →

PROTOPLANET: A stage in the formation of a planet where the planet is nearly complete. Protoplanets are generally round and have a core, mantle, and crust, but are still growing by attracting nearby planetesimals.

PROTOPLANETARY DISK: A rotating disk of dense gas that surrounds a newly formed star. As the components of a protoplanetary disk condense into larger bodies, the protoplanetary disk evolves into a debris disk and eventually into planets and moons.

REGOLITH: The layer of loose rock, soil, and dust on the surface of a terrestrial planet, moon, or asteroid. The fine dust covering the surface of the moon is regolith that was produced mainly by impacts with meteoroids.

THE SOLAR SYSTEM

REGULAR SATELLITE: A moon that orbits a planet in a nearly circular orbit over the planet's equator. Regular satellites probably formed at the same time the planet did from the protoplanetary disk. Irregular satellites have other types of orbits and were probably traveling through space until they were captured by the planet's gravity.

RETROGRADE MOTION: Planets and stars normally move from east to west in the night sky, but sometimes a planet that is farther away from the sun than Earth is, such as Mars or Jupiter, will appear to slow down in the sky, then go backward for a few months, then start moving forward again. This is called retrograde motion and is an illusion caused when the faster-moving Earth passes up the slower-moving superior planet.

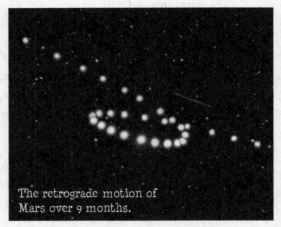

The retrograde motion of Mars over 9 months.

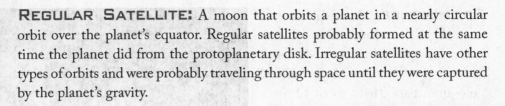

The next time you are riding in a car, watch for slower-moving cars on your right. When they are still ahead of you, they seem to be moving forward against the background, but as you pass them they seem to be moving backward against the background. Once they're behind you, they appear to be moving forward again against the background. This is retrograde motion, and is the same thing that happens when Earth passes a slower-moving planet.

REVOLUTION: One complete orbit of one object around another. The Earth completes one revolution around the sun in one year. The moon completes one revolution around the Earth in about 29 days. This is also called *orbital period*.

REVOLVE: To move around another object in an elliptical orbit. Planets, comets, and the main belt asteroids revolve around the sun. Moons revolve around their host planets.

ROCHE LIMIT: The closest distance a body can come to a planet without being pulled apart by the planet's gravity. A planet's moons and rings are all outside its Roche limit, because any moons that might have drifted closer would have been torn apart.

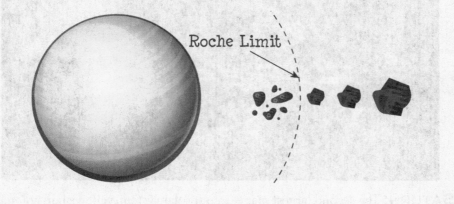

Roche Limit

We tried to warn you, but did you listen? In 1992, Comet Shoemaker-Levy 9 passed within Jupiter's Roche limit and was broken into 21 pieces that then crashed into the planet.

ROTATE: Another word for *spin*. The Earth rotates on an axis that runs from the North Pole to the South Pole.

ROTATION: The spin of an object around its central axis. Earth completes one rotation every 24 hours.

SAROS CYCLE: Lunar eclipses and solar eclipses occur at regular intervals that are 18 years, 11 days, and 8 hours apart. This period of time is called a Saros cycle.

SATELLITE: Any object that orbits a larger body. A moon is a natural satellite, and Earth is also orbited by many man-made satellites that relay information to and from Earth, such as telephone transmissions, television, weather information, and GPS navigation. There are currently about 1,100 active satellites in orbit around Earth, plus another 2,600 that no longer work.

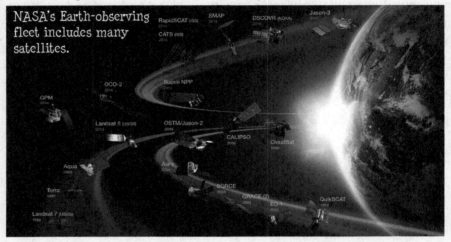

NASA's Earth-observing fleet includes many satellites.

SATURN: The second largest planet in our solar system, yellowish in color and known for its ring system. Saturn is a gas giant like Jupiter, composed primarily of hydrogen and helium, and is a ball of gases without a solid surface. Saturn's rings are made almost entirely of water ice, along with some small rocky debris and dust. Saturn's rings begin about 4,100 miles (about half of the diameter of Earth) above the planet's surface, and extend 75,000 miles (or nearly eight Earth diameters) into space.

That's a big beach ball! Saturn is the least dense of all the planets. If you could find a swimming pool big enough to throw it into, Saturn would float.

SECONDARY ATMOSPHERE: A secondary atmosphere is a planetary atmosphere that did not form directly from the protoplanetary disk at the same time the planet itself was being formed. A secondary atmosphere forms from gases leaking out of the planet through volcanic activity and by the accumulation of material from comet and asteroid impacts. Secondary atmospheres are much less dense than primary atmospheres. Venus, Earth, and Mars all have secondary atmospheres.

Secondary atmosphere escapes from the interior.

SHEPHERD MOON: Ringed planets sometimes have moons that orbit near or even within the rings, and the gravitational pull of these shepherd moons helps hold the material of the rings in place. All of the outer planets in our solar system have shepherd moons.

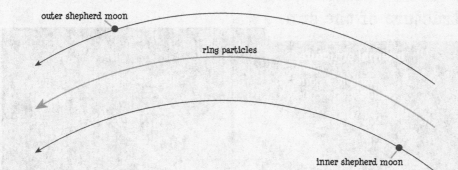

outer shepherd moon

ring particles

inner shepherd moon

SHOOTING STAR: Another name for *meteor*.

SHORT-PERIOD COMET: A comet that orbits the sun at least once every 200 years. Halley's Comet with a 76-year orbital period is the best-known short-period comet.

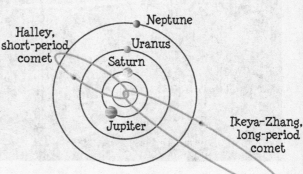

Halley, short-period comet

Neptune

Uranus

Saturn

Jupiter

Ikeya-Zhang, long-period comet

SIDEREAL: Sidereal means based on distant stars. You'll sometimes see terms like *sidereal day* or *sidereal year*. Normally we measure time based on Earth's movement around the sun, but time can also be measured based on the positions of the stars. A sidereal day is 4 minutes shorter than a usual solar day. Astronomers use sidereal time when calculating where to point their telescopes to see faint, distant stars.

SMALL SOLAR SYSTEM BODY: Any natural, solid object in our solar system that isn't a planet, dwarf planet, or moon. This includes comets, asteroids, meteoroids, and Kuiper belt objects. They have irregular shapes because their gravity is not strong enough to pull them into a spherical shape.

SOL: The Latin name for the sun; a term used by planetary astronomers to describe a solar day on Mars.

SOLAR: Having to do with the sun.

Structure of the sun.

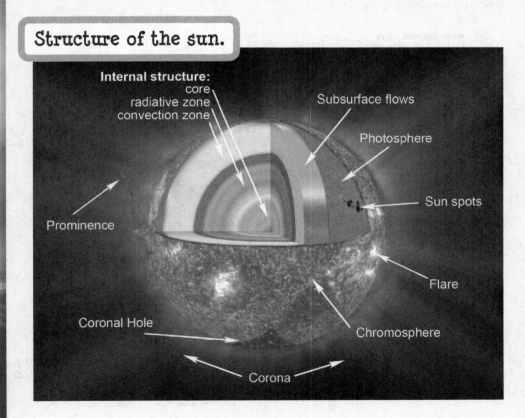

SOLAR CYCLE: A repeating cycle where the activity of the sun increases and decreases in a predictable pattern. The solar cycle is caused by a continual change in the sun's magnetic field, which controls surface activity including solar flares, sunspots, and coronal mass ejections. Each solar cycle lasts about 11 years, but they can be as short as 9 years or as long as 13.

These images from 1991 to 2001 demonstrate the variation in solar activity during a solar cycle.

SOLAR ECLIPSE: A solar eclipse occurs when the moon passes between the Earth and the sun and blocks out the sun. A solar eclipse can only happen during a new moon, when the moon is out during the daytime.

THE SOLAR SYSTEM

THE SOLAR SYSTEM

SOLAR FLARE: A sudden outward eruption on the sun's surface that shows up as a flash of brightness usually lasting less than one hour. Solar flares are the largest explosions in the solar system, but they are not visible to the naked eye and can only be seen using specialized equipment.

The energy released by an average solar flare is equal to more than a billion nuclear bombs exploding all at once.

SOLAR MAXIMUM: The point in the solar cycle where sunspot activity is at its peak and the output of radiation and particles from solar flares is highest. During Solar Cycle 23, which lasted from 1995 to 2008, there was a peak of 120 sunspots per month during the solar maximum.

SOLAR MINIMUM: The point in the solar cycle where sunspot activity is quietest and the output of radiation and particles from solar flares is lowest. During the solar minimum, days at a time can pass with no solar flares. During the solar minimum of the Solar Cycle 23 (1995 to 2008), there was an average of less than two sunspots per day or 60 per month, with more than 800 days that had no sunspots at all.

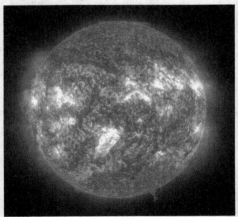

Solar maximum
from July 19, 2000

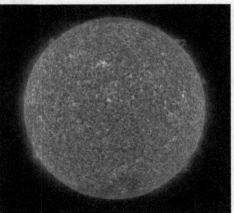

Solar minimum
from March 18, 2009

SOLAR NEBULA: A nebula is a large cloud of dust and gas in space. The solar nebula is the nebula from which our solar system formed about 4.6 billion years ago.

SOLAR SYSTEM: The sun and all of the celestial bodies that are caught within the sun's gravitational pull. In addition to the sun, the eight planets, and their moons, our solar system includes asteroids, comets, and meteoroids. The solar system is usually considered to end at the heliopause (the point where the solar wind from the sun ends), which occurs past the Kuiper belt but before the Oort cloud. The Oort cloud is still bound by the sun's gravity but is also affected by the gravity of objects passing by outside of our solar system.

SOLAR WIND: A stream of high-energy, electrically charged particles (mostly protons and electrons) that flows outward from the sun in all directions at speeds of more than a million miles per hour. The solar wind is what causes comet tails to point away from the sun. When the solar wind reaches Earth it causes the northern and southern lights.

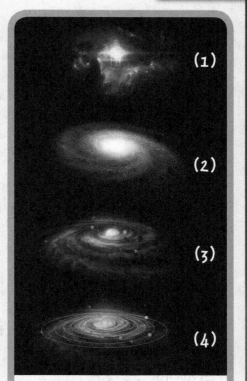

(1)
(2)
(3)
(4)

Solar system formation.
(1) Solar nebula (2) Gravity draws the solar nebula into a flat, rotating disk, bringing dust particles closer together. (3) Dust grains collide and stick together, forming larger clumps of matter. Through repeated collisions, moon-sized planetesimals are formed—the solar system is a chaotic swirl of countless small bodies in a cloud of gas. (4) Solar wind from the newly-forming sun in the center blows the gases away into space. Some planetesimals are thrown out of the system by collisions and gravity, some find a stable orbit around the sun, and others continue to grow, forming planets and moons.

SOLSTICE: The 2 days each year when the sun appears farthest north or south of the celestial equator. In the Northern Hemisphere, the summer solstice falls between June 20–22, and the winter solstice falls between December 20–23. These mark the first day of summer and the first day of winter. (In the Southern Hemisphere the seasons are reversed, so winter begins in June and summer begins in December.) The summer solstice is the longest day of the year, and the winter solstice is the shortest day of the year.

STONY METEORITE: A meteorite that looks like an Earth rock and is made of similar materials. About 94 out of every 100 meteorites is a stony meteorite.

STONY-IRON METEORITE: Also called *siderolites*, these meteorites are made of both rock and iron in roughly equal amounts. These are very rare. Fewer than 300 have been found so far.

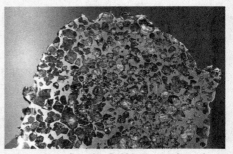

An example of a Pallasite meteorite, a type of stony-iron meteorite.

SUN: The star at the center of our solar system. Like all stars, the sun is made up almost entirely of hydrogen and helium, and generates heat and light through a process called fusion in which small atoms are pressed together to form larger ones. The sun formed around the same time as the rest of our solar system, about 4.6 billion years ago, and makes up 99.8% of the mass of the entire solar system—this means the sun weighs almost 500 times as much as everything else in the solar system combined. The sun is 93 million miles away from Earth (150 million kilometers), and has a diameter about 110 times larger than Earth's.

Star light, star bright! Our sun is a type of star called a *yellow dwarf* (p. 57), and is brighter than 90% of the stars in the Milky Way galaxy.

Plenty of fusion left in me! The sun is about halfway through its 10 billion year life expectancy.

SUNSPOT: A dark patch on the surface of the sun that is not as hot as the areas around it. Although they appear fairly small on the sun, sunspots are often planet-sized in diameter. They are caused by changes in the sun's magnetic field, and usually appear in pairs. Sunspots can generate solar flares that send bursts of charged particles hurling toward Earth at more than a million miles an hour and can disrupt communication satellites and power grids on Earth.

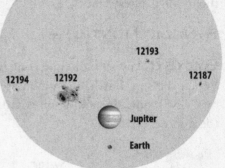

By Jove, that's a sunspot! Sunspot AR 12192 appeared for a few weeks in October 2014 and was the size of Jupiter. It was the largest sunspot seen in 24 years.

SUNSPOT CYCLE: See *Solar Cycle*, p. 107.

SUPERIOR CONJUNCTION: When Mercury or Venus is on the exact opposite side of the sun from Earth so that Earth, the sun, and the other planet all fall in a straight line.

SUPERIOR PLANET: A planet whose orbit lies farther from the sun than Earth's orbit. Mars, Jupiter, Saturn, Uranus, and Neptune are all superior planets. Sometimes the term superior planet is used to mean any planet whose orbit is larger than the orbit of the planet you're talking about: for example, Earth is a superior planet to Venus, and all of the other planets are superior to Mercury. (See *Inferior Planet*, p. 82.)

SUPERMOON: Because the moon's orbit around Earth is elliptical, sometimes the moon is closer to Earth than other times. If there is a full moon when the moon is at its closest point to Earth, the moon appears larger and brighter than normal. This is called a supermoon.

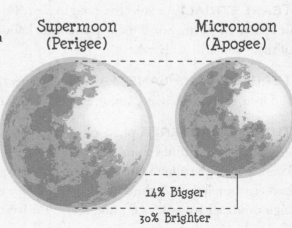

Supermoon (Perigee)

Micromoon (Apogee)

14% Bigger

30% Brighter

THE SOLAR SYSTEM

SYNCHRONOUS ROTATION: The moon takes about 29 days to complete one orbit around the Earth, and it also takes the same amount of time to make one complete revolution on its axis. When the time it takes to complete one orbit is the same as the time required to complete one rotation, that's called synchronous rotation. The result of synchronous rotation is that the same side of the moon is always facing Earth.

SYNODIC MONTH: See *Lunar Month*, p. 88.

SYZYGY: Any straight-line configuration of three bodies in the solar system. When the sun, Earth, and moon are in syzygy, we will have either a full moon or a new moon, depending on whether the moon is at the end of the line or in the middle.

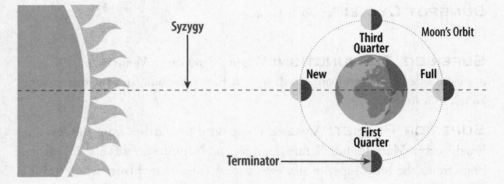

TERMINATOR: The boundary line between day and night on any celestial object. When you see a half moon in the sky, the straight side is the terminator.

TERRESTRIAL: An adjective used to describe anything originating on Earth or related to Earth. Small rocky planets are known as terrestrial planets because of their similarity to Earth.

TERRESTRIAL PLANET: Any small planet that is composed mainly of rock and iron, such as Mercury, Venus, Earth, and Mars.

THIRD QUARTER: A phase of the moon that is half lit by the sun and half in shadow as it shrinks from a full moon toward a new moon. In the Northern Hemisphere, the illuminated part of a third quarter moon is shaped like a backward capital D. A third quarter moon rises in the east around midnight, is high overhead around 6 a.m., and sets in the west around noon.

TIDAL FORCE: The entire moon does not feel the same gravitational pull from the Earth because gravity is weaker at farther distances. So the points on the moon that are closest to Earth feel a stronger gravitational pull than the points that are farther away. This difference in pulling force felt by an object is called tidal force. When tidal forces are large they can deform objects, cause them to heat up inside, or even tear them apart.

Warmer on the inside! Jupiter's moons show evidence of being heated inside from tidal forces due to Jupiter's gravity. Europa has an icy exterior, but contains liquid water under the surface where it is warmer. Tidal forces have heated Io even more, giving it a mantle made of molten rock and a surface covered with active volcanoes.

Europa

Io

TITAN: Saturn's largest moon. Titan is larger than the planet Mercury, is made up mostly of rock and ice, and has seas of liquid methane on its surface. Titan's atmosphere is made up almost entirely of nitrogen gas, but contains thick yellow smog that hides the surface of the moon from view.

TRANSIT: The passage of a smaller body in front of a much larger one, such as Venus passing in front of the sun, where the smaller object does not eclipse the larger one, but covers only a small area of it.

THE SOLAR SYSTEM

TRANS-NEPTUNIAN OBJECT (TNO): Any object that orbits the sun somewhere beyond the orbit of Neptune. This includes objects in the Kuiper belt and the Oort cloud.

> **Flip-flop!** Once every 248 years Pluto's orbit crosses Neptune's, and Pluto sneaks in closer to the sun than Neptune, until Pluto crosses back again 20 years later. The last time this happened was February 7, 1979, to February 11, 1999. But even when Pluto is closer to the sun than Neptune is, Pluto is still considered a TNO because its average orbital distance is greater than Neptune's.

TRITON: Neptune has 14 moons, but Triton is the largest and makes up 99.7% of the mass of all of Neptune's moons combined. Triton is made of frozen gases around a rock and metal core. Because Triton orbits Neptune in the opposite direction of Neptune's rotation, it's possible that Triton is a captured Kuiper belt object that disrupted the orbit of Neptune's other moons, ejecting them from orbit and leaving only the 13 tiny moons that remain.

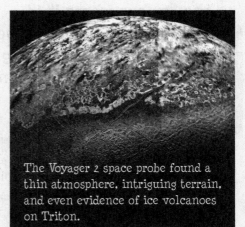

The Voyager 2 space probe found a thin atmosphere, intriguing terrain, and even evidence of ice volcanoes on Triton.

TROJAN: An object that orbits slightly ahead or slightly behind a larger object in the same orbit. There are two clusters of Trojan asteroids in Jupiter's orbit. One cluster is ahead of Jupiter and one is behind, and the distance from the leading Trojans to the trailing Trojans is about a third of Jupiter's orbit. There are about as many asteroids in Jupiter's orbit as there are in the main belt.

UMBRA: The dark central region of a shadow. When the moon passes through the Earth's umbra, there is a total lunar eclipse.

URANUS: The third largest planet in the solar system and an ice giant like Neptune. Uranus is tipped over on its side, so at various times its north and south poles point directly toward the sun as it goes through its 84-year-long orbit around the sun. Uranus has a pale blue color because of the methane gas in its upper atmosphere.

> **. . . Mars, Jupiter, Saturn, George . . .** When William Herschel discovered Uranus in 1781, he wanted to name it after England's King George III.

VAN ALLEN BELTS: The Earth is surrounded by two layers of electrically charged particles that came from the solar wind and are trapped in space by Earth's magnetic field. These layers of charged particles are called the Van Allen belts. The Van Allen belts begin about 600 miles above Earth's surface and extend nearly 40,000 miles into space (about 1,000–60,000 km). The belts are made up mostly of protons and electrons, and are hazardous to satellites.

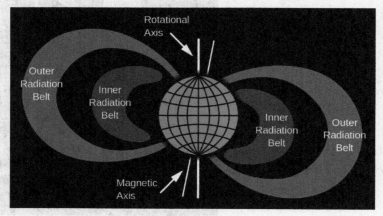

THE SOLAR SYSTEM

VENUS: A terrestrial planet that is slightly smaller than Earth. Venus is sometimes called Earth's sister planet because it is so close in size, but the two planets are very different. Venus has a thick atmosphere of carbon dioxide that traps heat and helps make Venus the hottest planet in our solar system, at nearly 900°F (480°C). Venus has thick clouds of sulfuric acid that reflect sunlight light and make Venus the second brightest object in the night sky after the moon. The sulfur in Venus's atmosphere is also what gives the planet its yellow color.

The forecast for tomorrow . . . cloudy! Venus appears to be the brightest star in the sky due to reflected sunlight—but the sunlight is not reflecting off the planet, it's bouncing off the thick atmosphere that surrounds Venus. The atmosphere on Venus is so thick that you can't actually see the planet with an optical telescope.

WANING: We say the moon is waning when the lit portion that we can see is shrinking from a gibbous moon down to a crescent moon as it goes from a full moon to a new moon.

WAXING: We say the moon is waxing when the lit portion that we can see is growing from a crescent moon to a gibbous moon on its way to being a full moon.

First Quarter
Waxing Gibbous
Waxing Crescent
Full
New
Waning Gibbous
Waning Crescent
Third Quarter

ZODIACAL LIGHT: A faint white glow that can sometimes be seen above the horizon in the direction of the sun before sunrise or after sunset. It is caused by sunlight that is scattered by space dust in the plane of the solar system, but it is so faint that it is washed out by moonlight or outdoor lighting. Zodiacal light is most easily seen before sunrise in the spring and after sunset in the fall.

A busy night sky! This 2014 image shows Venus and a band of zodiacal light on the left. The central band of the Milky Way appears as well, with a streak of a meteor on the right. The bright spot to the left of the meteor is the plume of an Ariane 5 rocket launching from Kourou, French Guiana.

THE SOLAR SYSTEM

ASTROBIOLOGY AND EXOPLANETS

IS THERE ANYBODY OUT THERE?

From the earliest days of astronomy, mankind has always been alone in the universe. Exoplanets—planets outside of our own solar system—existed only in the imaginations of science fiction writers, along with the alien creatures who lived there, whether they were friendly, helpful aliens, or aggressive invaders determined to conquer Earth.

Then, in 1992, the invasion began—but it wasn't aliens invading Earth—it was astronomers invading science fiction. In 1992, the discovery of two exoplanets, first detected 4 years earlier, was confirmed and announced to the public. Alien worlds outside our solar system were no longer the sole property of science fiction writers. More than that, the alien worlds described by the astronomers were actually real.

As many as 5,000 more exoplanets have been discovered since then. Most are somewhere between Earth-sized and Neptune-sized planets, and all of them are probably uninhabitable by any form of life as we know it. The search for habitable exoplanets continues side-by-side with another intrusion into science fiction: the search for extraterrestrial life.

The SETI Project (Search for Extraterrestrial Intelligence) has been scanning the skies for decades, searching for faint radio signals that are not natural in origin. These could be the equivalent of radio and television broadcasts like those used on Earth, but which have traveled light-years through space and might be detected by our antennae. Our own early radio and television broadcasts have now reached more than 50 light-years into space.

Closer to home, evidence of liquid water has been found on the surface of Mars and under the surface of two of Jupiter's moons, Europa and Ganymede, as well as beneath one of Saturn's moons, Enceladus. Extraterrestrial water in the form of ice or vapor has been found in 19 more places throughout the solar system. Where there's water there may be life, or there may once have been life.

The astronomers' invasion of science fiction continues, as the scientific search intensifies for life elsewhere in our solar system. Missions are already underway to gather more data on whether the conditions on Mars or beneath the surface of Jupiter's moons could ever have supported life, and if any traces of ancient extraterrestrial life remain—or even if life is there still.

The words presented in this section are related to exoplanets and alien life. Some of the terms in this section involve extraordinary life forms that are found on Earth. The discovery of these creatures shows that life is more adaptable to harsh environments than we ever expected—maybe even on a planet or moon with no oxygen.

AMINO ACIDS: Simple molecules that are present in all life on Earth. Amino acids connect together end-to-end like train cars to form long chains called *proteins*. All life as we know it requires amino acids, so any discovery of amino acids in space opens up the possibility that there might be life there as well.

Mighty molecule!
Alanine is a simple amino acid that is found in many proteins.

ANAEROBE: An organism that does not require oxygen to live—and may even be poisoned by oxygen. On Earth most anaerobes are single-celled bacteria, but three species of larger, multi-cellular anaerobic organisms were found living at the bottom of the Mediterranean Sea in 2010.

ASTROBIOLOGY: The study of life in outer space as well as on Earth. Astrobiology includes determining the origins, evolution, and distribution of life in the universe. Studying life on Earth provides clues as to what we might expect to find if and when we discover life elsewhere in the universe.

BIOMARKER: An indication of the existence of life even when there is no life present. A fossil is one example of a biomarker. Astrobiologists look for biomarkers of microscopic life in meteorites.

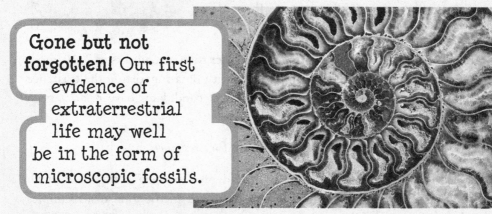

Gone but not forgotten! Our first evidence of extraterrestrial life may well be in the form of microscopic fossils.

CYANOBACTERIA: Sometimes called blue-green algae (even though they are not algae), cyanobacteria are a class of bacteria that create oxygen through photosynthesis. Scientists believe that Earth's atmosphere had very little oxygen gas in it until cyanobacteria evolved and began photosynthesizing. They transformed Earth's atmosphere into one that could support the kinds of life we see today. If we find an exoplanet with an oxygen-rich atmosphere, there will likely be some form of life similar to cyanobacteria living there.

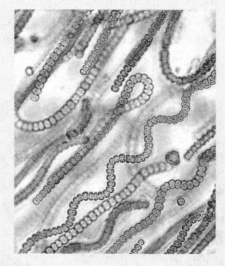

ENZYME: A special kind of protein that helps carry out chemical reactions that are necessary for life. Enzymes are essential to all life on Earth, and it's likely that they would be essential to any form of alien life as well.

ASTROBIOLOGY AND EXOPLANETS

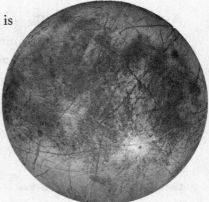

EUROPA: One of Jupiter's moons, Europa is believed to have an underground ocean of liquid water that is larger than all of Earth's oceans combined. Scientists believe that Europa might be the most promising place for finding life elsewhere in our solar system. NASA is planning a mission to Jupiter in the 2020s that would include 45 flybys of Europa to examine it more closely to try to determine if Europa's underground oceans can (or do) support life.

EXOPLANET: A planet that orbits a star other than our sun. As of 2016, more than 3,000 exoplanets have been discovered, with data supporting the existence of about 2,000 more, but these 2,000 exoplanet candidates have not yet been confirmed.

EXTRASOLAR PLANET: Another term for *exoplanet*.

EXTREMOPHILE: An organism that has adapted to living in extremely harsh environments. All of the extremophiles on Earth are microorganisms. Examples include hyperthermophiles, which can live at temperatures up to 250°F (122°C); anaerobes, which do not require oxygen to live; and xerophiles, which can live in extremely dry conditions. The existence of extremophiles on Earth suggests that there may be life even in harsh environments on exoplanets where we normally might not expect anything to survive.

Yellowstone National Park is home to thermophiles, which can live at temperatures up to 250°F. Do you think even more resilient extremophiles might be found on other planets?

HABITABLE ZONE: Also known as the Goldilocks Zone, the Habitable Zone is a narrow range of distance from a star in which liquid water exists on the surface of a planet and makes it more likely that planet can support life. The Habitable Zone for any planet will depend on the type of star it is orbiting as well as the size, composition, and atmosphere of the planet.

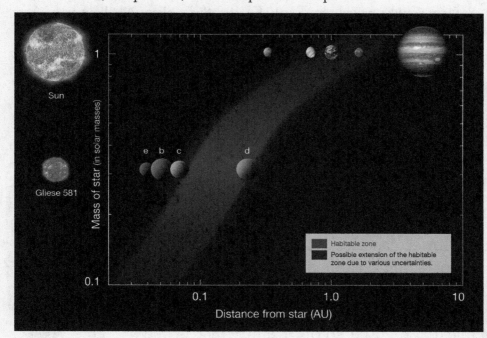

HOT JUPITER: A large gas giant planet similar to Jupiter that orbits very close to its parent star.

KEPLER SPACE TELESCOPE: An orbiting observatory that was specifically designed to find exoplanets. Kepler's photometer is a device that continually monitors the brightness of 145,000 stars looking for the periodic dimming that indicates a planet may be orbiting the star. Most of the exoplanets discovered so far have been found using data from Kepler.

KEPLER-186F: The first confirmed Earth-size exoplanet that orbits in its star's habitable zone. Kepler-186f is slightly larger than Earth and is believed to be a rocky planet, but this is not certain. One year on Kepler-186f is 130 days long. Kepler-186f orbits about as close to its star as Mercury is from the sun, but because Kepler-186f's star is much dimmer than the sun, daylight on Kepler-186f is more like twilight on Earth. Kepler-186f is about 490 light-years from Earth in the constellation Cygnus.

Why do they call it that? When an exoplanet is discovered, it is given a designation, or temporary name, that has two parts. The first part of the designation is typically the star that the exoplanet orbits or the instrument or scientific project that discovered the exoplanet. The second part is a lower case letter. The first exoplanet discovered orbiting a particular star will have a designation ending in "a," and if another planet is discovered orbiting the same star, it will end in "b," and so on. Kepler-186f is the sixth exoplanet discovered orbiting the star Kepler-186.

MICROLENSING: Sometimes the light from a star is bent by the gravity of an exoplanet that is between us and the star. Although we can't see the planet, we can calculate its position and mass based on how much it bends the light from its star. Microlensing allows us to detect small exoplanets with masses just a few times greater than Earth's, as well as planets that orbit very dim or distant stars.

MINI-NEPTUNE: An ice planet that is larger than Earth but smaller than Neptune. Mini-Neptunes are the most common type of exoplanet discovered so far.

PANSPERMIA: The hypothesis that life exists throughout the universe and is spread from one planet or star system to another by meteoroids, asteroids, comets, and planetoids. So far, no evidence has been found to suggest that this is true, but for many astrobiologists it remains a possibility.

SEARCH FOR EXTRATERRESTRIAL INTELLIGENCE (SETI): A collective term for a variety of different scientific projects aimed at determining if there is intelligent life in. SETI projects search the skies for radio signals or other indications of advanced civilizations elsewhere in the galaxy.

Some SETI data comes from the VLA (p. 129).

SUPER-EARTH: An extrasolar planet with a mass of less than about 10 Earth masses. The term super-Earth only refers to mass, and does not mean the planet resembles Earth in any way. If a super-Earth is known to be an ice planet or a gas planet, it might be referred to as a mini-Neptune or a gas dwarf instead.

TARDIGRADE: Also known as water bears, tardigrades are almost microscopic, eight-legged animals no more than about 1.5 mm long that normally live in water but are capable of surviving in an extraordinary range of conditions. For example, they can survive temperatures ranging from nearly absolute zero to above the boiling point of water (-450°F to 300°F). They can also withstand radiation that is hundreds of times above a lethal dose for humans. They can survive in the vacuum of outer space, and can survive inactive without food or water for more than 10 years. When placed back in water, they soak it up like a sponge and then go on with their lives. Tardigrades are not considered extremophiles because although they can survive these conditions, they are not adapted to thrive under them. But their ability to survive such a range of conditions makes it more believable that life could spread from one planet to another on meteoroids.

ASTROBIOLOGY AND EXOPLANETS

TERRAFORMING: Changing a planet to make it more easily inhabitable by humans. This could mean changing the atmosphere, temperature, surface, and ecology of a planet, moon, or other body in space to make it more like Earth.

TITAN: Saturn's largest moon has lakes of methane on its surface, and is the only body in our solar system other than Earth that contains any kind of liquid on its surface. The existence of liquid methane raises the question of whether Titan might be home to life forms unlike anything on Earth.

TRANSIT: The passing of a smaller body, such as a planet, in front of a much larger body, such as a star. The first exoplanets were discovered by measuring the repeated dimming of light from some distant stars as large exoplanets orbiting those stars passed between the star and Earth and blocked some of the light from the star.

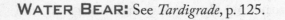

WATER BEAR: See *Tardigrade*, p. 125.

A History
of Space
Exploration

Humans explore space in three different ways: (1) by looking out into space from Earth or from telescopes that orbit Earth, (2) by sending unmanned probes out into space to analyze and photograph things close up, and (3) by sending people into space. This interactive chronological history of space exploration is told through entries roughly listed in order of increasing technology, which means the earlier efforts are listed first, leading up to the most modern missions, which are listed last.

Telescopes

Invented in the 1600s, the telescope revolutionized the field of astronomy, providing the first close-up views of the sky and beyond. There are many different kinds of telescopes. Optical telescopes, which include refracting telescopes and reflecting telescopes, allow us to see distant objects close up. Other types of telescopes, such as radio telescopes and X-ray telescopes, detect forms of light that are invisible to our eyes.

Modern telescopes include X-ray telescopes, gamma ray telescopes, and high-energy particle telescopes. These are all satellites that are placed in orbit around Earth to detect specific types of energy coming from distant objects in space. Although the Hubble Space Telescope is the most famous telescope in space, there are actually dozens of smaller space telescopes in orbit around Earth.

✧ **OBSERVATORY:** Normally this refers to a building that houses a large telescope. These ground-based observatories have rounded domes on top, which can be opened and rotated so that the opening faces any direction in the sky. The telescope is aimed out through the opening and rotates with the dome. Observatories are usually located far away from the lights of a city, and often on mountains or higher elevations to minimize interference from Earth's atmosphere. Telescopes can also be placed on high-flying airplanes (airborne observatories) or in orbit around Earth (space observatories).

✧ **REFRACTING TELESCOPES:** The first telescopes, invented in 1609. Refracting telescopes use two pieces of curved glass called *lenses* inside a long tube to magnify a distant object. The biggest problems with refracting telescopes are that tiny imperfections in the glass lenses cause the images to be fuzzy or distorted, and getting greater magnification requires building an extremely large telescope. Astronomers solved these problems by inventing the reflecting telescope, which replaces the glass lenses with curved mirrors.

✧ **REFLECTING TELESCOPES:** Using curved mirrors instead of glass lenses allowed astronomers to make telescopes that capture more light and produce clearer images. In 1668, Isaac Newton proved that reflecting telescopes can work, but the first truly successful reflecting telescope wasn't built until 1673. Most of the optical telescopes used in space research today, including the optical telescope on the Hubble Space Telescope, are reflecting telescopes.

✧ **RADIO TELESCOPES:** These look like giant-sized satellite dishes instead of tubes to look through. Radio telescopes are not optical telescopes and don't detect visible light. They are used to detect and study objects in space such as pulsars and quasars whose emissions reach Earth as radio waves instead of visible light.

Perspici-what? Before they were called telescopes, Galileo called his telescope a *perspicillum.*

VERY LARGE ARRAY (VLA; 1980):
A collection of 27 radio telescopes spread out over 5 square miles (13 square kilometers) in New Mexico. Each of the radio telescopes is 82 feet (25 meters) in diameter, and working together they are able to detect faint signals that one radio telescope alone could not. The VLA has been used to study black holes, the formation of new solar systems, and the center of our galaxy.

HUBBLE SPACE TELESCOPE (HST; 1990): Launched in 1990 and about the size of a school bus, the HST is a satellite telescope that orbits Earth and has taken the best photos we have so far of distant objects in space. The Hubble has provided images of objects as far as 13.2 billion light-years away.

These high-resolution images taken by the Hubble Space Telescope show a bright star that is actually a binary star system (p. 23). You can see this in the close-up pictures at the bottom and bottom right.

CHANDRA X-RAY OBSERVATORY (1993): An orbiting X-ray telescope that measures X-rays coming from objects such as neutron stars and black holes. It was launched in 1993 with an expected 5-year lifetime, but it is still operational in 2016. The telescope is named in honor of Indian-American astrophysicist Subrahmanyan Chandrasekhar, whose friends called him Chandra.

HISTORY OF SPACE EXPLORATION

LASER INTERFEROMETER GRAVITATIONAL-WAVE OBSERVATORY (LIGO; 2002): LIGO is a land-based observatory made up of two underground mirror systems that are designed to detect gravitational waves. One system is located in Washington and the other is in Louisiana. In 2016, LIGO scientists announced the first successful measurement of gravitational waves coming off a collision between two black holes about 1.3 billion light-years away.

Louisiana Washington

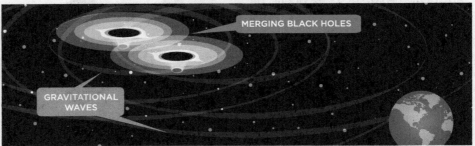

MERGING BLACK HOLES

GRAVITATIONAL WAVES

KEPLER SPACE OBSERVATORY (2009): Launched in 2009, Kepler is designed specifically for finding exoplanets. Kepler continually monitors the brightness of more than 145,000 stars in a specific region of the sky that includes parts of the constellations Cygnus, Lyra, and Draco. The brightness data is sent to Earth and analyzed to look for any repeated dimming and brightening patterns in the stars that might be caused by an exoplanet passing in front of a star and blocking some of its light. From 2009 to 2016, Kepler discovered more than 1,000 confirmed exoplanets, although nearly all of them are large and uninhabitable by humans. Only eight of the exoplanets are less than twice the mass of Earth and also in their star's habitable zone. Although Kepler was only intended to operate for 3–4 years, as of 2016 it has been working for 7 years and is still operational.

JAMES WEBB SPACE TELESCOPE (JWST; 2018): A space telescope that is currently scheduled to launch in October 2018. The JWST is designed to learn more about what the universe was like shortly after the Big Bang, and also learn more about how galaxies, stars, and planets form. In order to do this, the JWST will be able to detect a wider range of infrared light than the Hubble Space Telescope can, and also has a light collection area five times greater than the Hubble's. The JWST will not orbit Earth as other space telescopes do, instead it will orbit the sun alongside the Earth in the Earth's shadow.

13.7 BILLION YEARS: PRESENT DAY

9 BILLION YEARS: OUR SUN FORMS

A FEW BILLION YEARS: QUASAR ERA

A FEW HUNDRED MILLION YEARS: FIRST GALAXIES

BIG BANG

1.5 million km from Earth

Eye into the past. The JWST will allow us to see farther distances than ever before, which means the objects we will be seeing are older than any objects ever seen. The JWST should be able to provide images of what the universe was like only 200 million years after the Big Bang.

HISTORY OF SPACE EXPLORATION

SPACE PROBES

Space probes are unmanned, remote-controlled machines that are sent into space in order to take close-up photographs or make measurements of celestial objects. Probes are always designed with a specific primary mission in mind. All space probes launched so far have been designed to study objects in our solar system, but Voyager 1 has left the solar system and is expected to keep sending information back to Earth until 2025. The type of probe that is used for a particular mission depends on what kind of information is being sought. Five different types of probes have been used:

✧ **FLYBY:** A probe that flies past an astronomical body in space, but does not orbit it. Flybys are usually thousands of miles to hundreds of thousands of miles away from the planet or object they are studying at their closest point.

✧ **ORBITER:** A probe that orbits an astronomical body in space.

✧ **IMPACTOR:** A probe that is designed to collect data during its descent through the atmosphere before crashing into the planet.

✧ **LANDER:** A probe that lands safely on the surface of an astronomical body but remains in one place as it collects samples and data. When a probe is able to land successfully and continue collecting data, that is referred to as a soft landing, as opposed to the hard landing of an impactor.

✧ **ROVER:** A probe that lands safely on the surface of a planet and is able to move around on the surface to collect samples and data.

A whisper, then a shout. Landers and rovers are typically part of a two-part probe that includes an orbiter. The lander or rover sends signals to the nearby orbiter, and a more powerful transmitter on the orbiter sends the signals to Earth.

There have been so many probes launched into space that we can't even list them all here, but these are some of the most important ones. The year listed in parentheses is the launch date for each probe, but some of the probes took years to reach their target.

SPUTNIK 1 (1957): Launched by the Soviet Union on October 4, 1957, Sputnik (Russian for "satellite") was the first artificial satellite ever launched into space, and sparked a space race between the United States and the Soviet Union. Sputnik was about the size of a beach ball, and each orbit around the Earth took a little more than an hour and a half. Sputnik's mission was to provide data about the temperature and density of Earth's upper atmosphere. Sputnik's batteries lasted for 22 days, then it stopped sending signals. Sputnik continued to orbit the Earth for another 70 days after that, making a total of 1,440 trips around the Earth before it entered the atmosphere and burned up.

MARINER 2 (1962): When Mariner 2 flew by Venus, it became the first space probe to reach another planet. (Mariner 1, launched about month earlier, was destroyed 5 minutes after takeoff when its rocket went off course.) Mariner 2 provided information about the dense atmosphere of Venus and its 864°F average surface temperature, as well as better estimates of the masses of the moon and of Venus, and also a better measure of the distance from the Earth to the sun. We learned so much from Mariner 2 that a planned follow-up mission was canceled.

It's lonely in space. One of Mariner 2's missions was to determine how much cosmic dust is floating around in the solar system, to see if this would be a problem for future space missions. On its 3.5-month journey from Earth to Venus, it found exactly one speck of dust.

MARINER 3 AND MARINER 4 (1964): The first American probe sent to Mars failed early. Mariner 3's solar panels were protected during takeoff by a cover called a *shroud*, which was supposed to come off shortly after takeoff. But it didn't come off, so the solar panels could not open, and Mariner 3 ran out of power less than 9 hours after takeoff. NASA quickly changed the design of the shroud on Mariner 4 before its launch 23 days later, and its solar panels successfully opened. Mariner 4 reached Mars after a 7.5-month voyage and sent back a variety of data including the first ever close-up photos of the Martian surface.

VENERA 7 (1970): The first successful landing on another planet. Venera 7 was a Soviet probe that landed on the surface of Venus and sent back temperature data for 23 minutes. The surface temperature where Venera 7 landed was 887°F (475°C). The signal sent by the Venera 7 was weak, and scientists think the probe fell on its side when it landed. The Russian Venera program would go on to land seven more probes on the surface of Venus. Most of these lasted less than an hour in the harsh Venusian environment. Venera 13 survived the longest, at 2 hours and 7 minutes. *Venera* is the Russian word for "Venus."

LUNA 16 (1970): The Russian space program has never landed a person on the moon, but Luna 16 was an unmanned space probe that landed on the moon, collected a 101-gram sample of soil, and returned it to Earth. Luna 20 (1972) and Luna 24 (1974) also returned samples of lunar soil to Earth.

PIONEER 10 (1972): The first probe to study Jupiter close up, in November and December 1973. It continued on toward the edge of the solar system and was still providing data as late as 2002. Pioneer 10 was 80 AU from Earth in 2003 when its signal began fading and we lost contact with it.

PIONEER 11 (1973): The first probe to study Saturn up close, after flying by Jupiter and one of its moons. By the time Pioneer 11 reached Saturn, Voyager 1 and Voyager 2 were already past Jupiter and on their way toward Saturn. (Voyager 1 and Voyager 2 were launched 4 years later but were traveling much faster.) Scientists

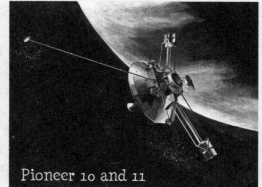
Pioneer 10 and 11

decided to fly Pioneer 11 through Saturn's rings to see if it sustained any damage. That way they would know if it was safe to fly the Voyager probes through the rings or whether they would have to steer around them. Pioneer 11 almost smashed into one of Saturn's minor moons within the rings but emerged unscathed, and the Voyager probes safely followed. Pioneer 11 went silent in 1996. As of 2016, Pioneer 11 would be about 93 AU from Earth.

MARINER 10 (1973): The first spacecraft to visit Mercury. Its mission was primarily to study the atmosphere and surface of Mercury and also collect data about Venus as it flew past. Mariner 10 provided the first close-up photos of Venus from space, as well as 2,800 photos of the surface of Mercury.

Hey, is that star? At one point on its way to Venus, a fleck of paint came off Mariner 10. The star tracker that was supposed to keep Mariner 10 on course detected the bright fleck of paint and plotted a new course based on the position of what it thought was a star. The problem was quickly corrected, but paint flecks were an ongoing problem for Mariner 10 after that.

VIKING 1 AND VIKING 2 (1976): The Viking probes were each made up of two parts. The orbiter circled Mars taking photos of Mars and its moons, while the lander landed on Mars to study the soil and look for water and organic chemicals that could be signs of life. The Viking program provided a wealth of new information about Mars, including the first photos taken at the surface of the planet, which helped make the later missions to Mars possible.

Martian junkyard! By the time the Viking probes landed on Mars, there was already the wreckage there of three failed Soviet probes. Between 1971 and 1974, the Soviet Union sent four probes to land on Mars. Mars 2 and Mars 6 crash-landed and were destroyed on impact. Mars 4 landed safely but stopped sending data less than 2 minutes later. Mars 7 malfunctioned in orbit and when it attempted to land on Mars, it missed the planet altogether.

VOYAGER 2 (1977): Launched in August 1977, Voyager 2's mission was to study Jupiter and Saturn, then fly by the ice giants Uranus and Neptune. Voyager 2 is still the only spacecraft ever to have visited Uranus and Neptune. As of 2016, Voyager 2 is about 110 AU from Earth, is still sending signals, and will soon enter interstellar space.

VOYAGER 1 (1977): Launched in September 1977, Voyager 1's mission was to study Jupiter, Saturn, and Saturn's largest moon Titan, then continue to the outer edge of the solar system. Voyager 1 left the solar system in 2012, and continues to send back data from interstellar space. Voyager 1 is expected to continue operating until 2025, when its power supply will finally give out.

GALILEO (1989): A probe sent to orbit Jupiter and study the planet, its moons, and its faint rings. Data from Galileo suggest there may be a liquid ocean under the surface of Jupiter's moon Europa. In 2003, after orbiting Jupiter for 8 years, Galileo was sent crashing into Jupiter to destroy it and prevent the possibility of contaminating Jupiter's moons with bacteria from Earth.

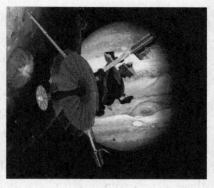

NEAR EARTH ASTEROID RENDEZVOUS-SHOEMAKER (NEAR-SHOEMAKER; 1996): The first probe to land on an asteroid, in 2001. NEAR-Shoemaker was designed to orbit the asteroid Eros and then send back photos as it slowly descended to the surface. As NEAR-Shoemaker's mission was coming to an end, NASA decided to try and land the probe on the asteroid, even though it was not designed for that. NEAR-Shoemaker then sent detailed data about the asteroid's surface for 2 more weeks before running out of power.

CASSINI–HUYGENS (1997): Cassini–Huygens did flybys of Earth, Venus, Jupiter, and Saturn before orbiting and landing on Saturn's largest moon, Titan, in January 2005. Cassini–Huygens was a joint effort by NASA, the European Space Agency, and the Italian Space Agency. The orbiter is named Cassini, and the lander is Huygens. As of 2016, Cassini–Huygens is still sending photos and data about Saturn's rings, moons, and atmosphere, but in 2017, Titan's gravity is expected to fling Cassini into Saturn's atmosphere and end the mission.

The little spacecraft that could. Voyager 1's computer has only 68 kilobytes of memory. A modern one-terabyte computer hard drive can store more than 10 million times as much data as Voyager 1 can.

SOJOURNER (1997): The first Mars rover, Sojourner was 2 feet long, 1 foot tall, and weighed about 25 pounds. Its 7-day mission was to analyze the atmosphere of Mars along with its rocks and soil, and take surface photos in black and white and in color. Sojourner ended up lasting 83 sols (or 85 days; see p. 106) instead of just 7, and traveled a total of 330 feet (100 meters) in that time.

SPIRIT AND OPPORTUNITY (2003): Much larger than Sojourner, these rovers were each 5 feet long, 5 feet tall, and weighed 400 pounds. The identical rovers were sent to opposite sides of Mars with a primary mission of looking for indications that there was once water on the surface of Mars. They found evidence that Mars once had salt water at the surface, but they were not equipped to search for fossils. Spirit got stuck in soft soil in 2009 and lost contact in 2010. As of 2016, Opportunity continues to study Mars, looking for features in the rocks and soil that might have been created by microbial life.

NEW HORIZONS (2006): The only spacecraft to make the 9-year journey to Pluto, New Horizons provided the first detailed photos of Pluto's surface in 2015. The primary mission of New Horizons is to study the surface and atmosphere of Pluto and its moon Charon, but New Horizons also did a flyby of Jupiter and its moons, and will visit the Kuiper belt. Its first encounter with a Kuiper belt object is expected to be on January 1, 2019. New Horizons carries about one ounce (about 30 grams) of Clyde Tombaugh's ashes. Tombaugh discovered Pluto in 1930.

New Horizons uses about one-fourth as much power as a two-slice toaster.

JUNO (2011): After a 5-year journey, Juno reached Jupiter in July 2016. Its mission is to orbit Jupiter and study Jupiter's composition, gravity, and magnetic field.

> **Behave yourself, Jupiter!**
> In Roman mythology, Juno was the name of Jupiter's angry, jealous wife and many of Jupiter's moons are named after his girlfriends, so it seems appropriate that a probe sent to watch over Jupiter would be named Juno.

CURIOSITY (2012): The largest Mars rover so far, Curiosity is about the size of a small car: almost 10 feet long, 7 feet tall, and weighing 2,000 pounds. Its mission is to continue studying the climate and geology of Mars, especially with regard to water and any evidence for life.

SPACE EXPLORERS

Telescopes and space probes are the safest ways to study objects in space, but just like on Earth, the way to learn the most about someplace is to go there yourself. Human exploration is the most dangerous and most expensive way to explore space, and the first space explorers were not people at all, but animals! Most of the manned space missions have not been designed to explore distant space in the same way telescopes and space probes do. Instead, astronauts usually conduct scientific experiments while in orbit around Earth so that some day in the future when we do send explorers on longer missions, they will be better prepared for success.

ANIMALS VENTURE INTO THE FINAL FRONTIER

LAIKA (1957): The first animal to orbit the Earth. She was a stray dog from the streets of Moscow and was sent into orbit aboard Sputnik 2 in November 1957 in a time when it was uncertain whether or not a human being could survive takeoff. Laika was supposed to orbit the Earth for 10 days, but a malfunction on board caused the space capsule to overheat and Laika died within a few hours of taking off. There is a statue in her honor in Moscow.

The writing at the top says, "Laika, the first traveler into the cosmos."

HAM THE ASTROCHIMP (1961): The first chimpanzee sent into space. Ham had been trained on Earth to pull a lever immediately after seeing a blue light, and scientists wanted to see if he was still able to do this in space. His response time was a little bit slower in space, but Ham showed that astronauts would be able to function in space much like they do on Earth. His 16-minute flight was in January 1961. After that, Ham lived until 1983 in the National Zoo in Washington, DC.

ENOS (1961): The first chimpanzee to orbit the Earth in November 1961, in a practice run for John Glenn orbiting the Earth aboard *Friendship* 7 that occurred 3 months later. Enos made two orbits of the Earth, each lasting about 90 minutes, before splashing down in the Atlantic Ocean. Enos died a year later from an unrelated infection.

Space Ark! Over the years, a wide array of animals have been sent into space, including monkeys, chimpanzees, dogs, cats, rats, mice, rabbits, guinea pigs, frogs, turtles, tortoises, geckos, newts, fish, snails, jellyfish, beetles, ants, cockroaches, fruit flies, and spiders.

HISTORY OF SPACE EXPLORATION

ASTRONAUTS AND SPACE PROGRAMS TAKE "ONE SMALL STEP FOR MAN . . ."

YURI GAGARIN (1961): The first person ever to go into space. He was a Russian cosmonaut who orbited the Earth in April 1961 on board the *Vostok 1* (Vostok is the Russian word for "east"). His flight was 108 minutes long and orbited the Earth once.

> **Just don't call me late for launch!**
> In English, we call space travelers *astronauts*, which comes from Greek words meaning "star sailor." In Russian, they are *cosmonauts*, and we call Chinese space travelers *taikonauts*.

PROJECT MERCURY (1961–1963): The first American space program, with the goal of launching an astronaut into orbit and retuning him safely to Earth. Unmanned missions began in 1959, with astronauts sent into space from 1961 to 1963. Each manned Mercury mission sent only one astronaut at a time into space. The seven astronauts in this program were known as the Mercury 7.

> **America's First Astronauts!**
> The Mercury 7 were (front row L-R): Wally Schirra, Deke Slayton, John Glenn, Scott Carpenter, and (back row L-R) Alan Shepard, Gus Grissom, and Gordon Cooper.

ALAN SHEPARD (1961): The first American in space in April 1961, in a 15-minute flight on board *Freedom 7* that sent him 116 miles up, then back down for a splashdown. In 1971, at the age of 47, Alan Shepard returned to space and walked on the moon as Commander of Apollo 14.

Fore! Alan Shepard hit two golf balls while on the moon.

JOHN GLENN (1962): The first American to orbit the Earth, in February 1962, on board the *Friendship 7*. His three-orbit flight lasted about 5 hours. John Glenn returned to space in 1998 at the age of 77, on board the Space Shuttle *Discovery*, making him the oldest person to have gone into space.

Don't say *Titanic*. Each of the pilots in the Mercury space program got to choose the name for his spacecraft, ending with a 7. The names they chose were *Freedom 7, Liberty Bell 7, Friendship 7, Aurora 7, Sigma 7,* and *Faith 7.* If you could name the spaceship that would take you into space, what would it be?

Wait, that was only six! You're right, only six Mercury spaceships were named because one of the Mercury 7 astronauts did not go into space . . . at least not with Project Mercury. Keep reading this section to see what happens later to astronaut Deke Slayton.

HISTORY OF SPACE EXPLORATION

PROJECT GEMINI (1961–1966): The second American space program, lasting from 1961 to 1966, Gemini had longer Earth orbit missions than Mercury did and was designed to learn what we needed to know in order to send an astronaut to the moon. Each Gemini mission carried two astronauts at a time.

APOLLO SPACE PROGRAM (1961–1972): The Apollo missions lasted from 1961 to 1972 and had the goal of landing astronauts on the moon and bringing them safely home. Apollo missions 2–6 were unmanned tests, but the other Apollo missions (Apollo 1 and Apollo 7–17) each carried three astronauts. On missions that included a moon landing, two of the astronauts walked on the moon and one stayed in orbit.

"The Snoopy has landed?" Apollo 10 was a practice run for Apollo 11's first moon landing. The command module of Apollo 10 was named Charlie Brown, and the lunar module was named Snoopy.

NEIL ARMSTRONG (1969): The first person to walk on the moon, on July 20, 1969. Buzz Aldrin walked the moon with him while Michael Collins remained in orbit piloting the Apollo command module.

They should have sent a cleaning crew! By the time the Apollo astronauts landed on the moon, there were already 18 abandoned American and Soviet lunar probes scattered across the moon's surface, dating back to 1959.

The Apollo 11 crew from left to right, Neil Armstrong, Michael Collins, and Buzz Aldrin.

The lucky dozen. Only 12 people have ever walked on the moon. The first was Neil Armstrong on Apollo 11 and the last person to leave was Apollo 17 commander Eugene Cernan. No one has ever gone back for a second time on the moon.

APOLLO-SOYUZ (1975): This joint space mission in 1975 marked the end of the space race and the beginning of American/Russian cooperation in space exploration. The American Apollo spacecraft docked in space with the Russian Soyuz spacecraft, and the astronauts and cosmonauts worked together on science experiments.

Worth the wait! Deke Slayton, the only one of the Mercury 7 astronauts who never went into space during the Mercury space program, finally got his chance as one of the Apollo astronauts on the 1975 Apollo-Soyuz mission. The longest Mercury flight was only about a day and a half long, but Slayton spent 9 days in space as part of Apollo-Soyuz.

SPACE SHUTTLE PROGRAM (1981–2011): Officially known as the Space Transportation System (STS), the space shuttles were the first reusable spaceships, and usually carried a crew of seven astronauts. They were intended to be used over a 10-year period to build and supply an American space station, but ended up being used over a 30-year period from 1981 to 2011 to help build the International Space Station instead. The space shuttles were also used for repairs on satellites and for carrying out scientific experiments. There were five space shuttles: *Columbia*, *Challenger*, *Discovery*, *Atlantis*, and *Endeavour*. (The first space shuttle, named *Enterprise*, was not capable of flying in space and was only used for test flights in the atmosphere.) A total of 135 space missions were flown by the space shuttles. *Challenger* exploded shortly after takeoff in 1986, and *Columbia* broke apart when reentering the atmosphere in 2003. Seven astronauts were killed in each of these disasters.

SALLY RIDE (1983): The first female American astronaut, and at age 32 was also the youngest American astronaut to go into space. Her first space flight was in 1983 on board the Space Shuttle *Challenger*. (Two female Russian cosmonauts went into space before Sally Ride did: Valentina Tereshkova in 1963 and Svetlana Savitskaya in 1982.) Sally Ride went into space again in 1984, once more on board the *Challenger*.

Eye in the sky. The *Discovery* carried the Hubble Space Telescope into space in April 1990. Later repairs to the Hubble were also carried out by Space Shuttle missions.

SPACE STATIONS

Space Stations are orbiting laboratories where people can live and work in space for weeks or even months. Space stations are used for carrying out longer scientific experiments and for testing the effects of long-term weightlessness on humans.

SALYUT 1 (1971): The first space station. The Soviet Union launched it into space in April 1971. Three days later, the first crew arrived in a separate rocket, but they were unable to dock with Salyut 1 and had to return to Earth. A second attempt in June was successful, and the three cosmonauts on that mission lived aboard Salyut 1 for 24 days. During their return to Earth, their ship lost pressure and all three men suffocated. No further missions were sent to Salyut 1, and it was taken out of orbit in October 1971.

SKYLAB (1973–1974): The first U.S. space station, Skylab was more than three times the size of Salyut 1. It was launched in May 1973. Between May of 1973 and February of 1974, three missions successfully docked with Skylab, bringing a total of nine astronauts to the space station. The astronauts on those three missions lived on Skylab for 28 days, 59 days, and 84 days respectively. After the third mission ended Skylab continued to orbit Earth for 5 years until July 1979, when it decayed out of orbit and broke apart on re-entry, with scattered pieces landing in Western Australia.

Knock, knock! Just in case anyone came visiting, the last crew to leave Skylab left the door unlocked.

MIR (1986–2001): The largest and most-visited space station until the International Space Station. Mir orbited the Earth for more than 15 years from 1986 to 2001, and was inhabited for more than 12 years during that time. Altogether 125 people lived and worked aboard Mir, usually three at a time. In March 2001, the aging space station was brought down from orbit. It burned and broke up on re-entry, with the pieces landing in the South Pacific Ocean.

INTERNATIONAL SPACE STATION (ISS; 1998–PRESENT):

Bigger than a football field and with three and a half times as much room inside as Skylab or Mir, the ISS is the largest space station ever put into orbit. It was launched in November 1998 and the first astronauts (one American and two Russians) arrived in November of 2000. The ISS has been continuously inhabited since then.

A whole new world. The ISS travels at 5 miles per second and orbits the Earth once every 90 minutes—the same amount of time it takes to watch Disney's *Aladdin*.

ISS's Orbit

52°

Equator

Don't go too far! More than 500 people have been to space, but only the 24 Apollo astronauts on moon missions have ever gone beyond Earth's orbit.

HISTORY OF SPACE EXPLORATION

147

AND BEYOND!

THE FUTURE OF PRIVATE SPACE TRAVEL

Throughout the 20th century, only governments of large nations could afford to develop space programs, but now many private companies are also beginning to provide services in space. These are just a few examples.

BIGELOW AEROSPACE (1999–PRESENT): A company based in Nevada that is developing inflatable rooms that can be attached to space stations to increase the living space available to astronauts.

BLUE ORIGIN (2000–PRESENT): A space travel company based in Washington state that is working to develop reusable spacecraft to make orbital space travel less expensive.

SPACEX (2002–PRESENT): A space travel company based in California that uses its unmanned Dragon spacecraft to send supplies to the International Space Station. SpaceX is currently developing Dragon V2, a reusable spacecraft that will be able to carry up to seven astronauts into orbit.

VIRGIN GALACTIC (2004–PRESENT): A company based in California that is working to provide space flights to tourists. These flights would go into space but not into orbit. Although the first flight is not yet scheduled, by the end of 2015 more than 700 people had already bought tickets. Virgin Galactic's long-range plans include orbital flights.

ORBITAL ATK (2015–PRESENT): A company based in Virginia that makes an unmanned cargo ship that is used for delivering supplies to the International Space Station.

> **Ticket to ride!** In 2016, the ticket price for a quick trip into space with Virgin Galactic was $250,000.

ASTRONOMY TIMELINE

When you think of a fortuneteller, you don't normally picture a scientist, but in a way that's exactly what scientists are. One of the main goals of science is to be able to predict the future. Scientists make observations and conduct experiments and then use the information they gain to develop theories. If a theory is able to predict the outcome of new experiments before they are carried out, then the theory is regarded as valid, but if the theory's predictions are wrong, then the theory is modified or discarded.

It should come as no surprise, then, that astronomy is the oldest science. Stone-age civilizations around the world studied the stars in the night skies thousands of years ago and found repeating patterns in what they saw. These patterns allowed hunters to predict when the moon would be full again and when the night sky would be moonless. Farming civilizations learned how to predict the changing of the seasons, and created calendars to help determine the best time to plant crops. Early astronomers saw repeating patterns in the positions of the stars, the phases of the moon, and even in the movements of the five "wandering stars" called planets. Many ancient civilizations, including the Greeks, Middle Easterners, and Mayans, developed their knowledge of astronomical patterns to the point where they were able to predict eclipses.

But not everything in the night sky was predictable. Sometimes without warning a bright new light would appear for weeks or months, something that looked like a large star but with a long, flowing tail of light. It made sense to early astronomers that if the stars could be used to predict the future, then these unexpected new stars must be predicting something as well. Because the early astronomers had no explanation for where these strange new stars came from, people's imaginations took over and the appearance of a comet was almost always regarded as an evil omen. The first sight of a comet could fill people with fear—they were convinced that something bad was about to happen, but they didn't know what. The early Chinese astronomers referred to comets as "vile stars."

A comet appeared shortly before Julius Caesar was assassinated in 59 B.C. Halley's Comet appeared in 1066 before the English king Harold Godwinson lost the Battle of Hastings to William the Conqueror. Two comets were seen over England in 1664 and 1665, and within months came the Great Plague of London, which killed almost 100,000 people over the next 2 years. Comets were routinely blamed for harmful natural events such as earthquakes, volcanic eruptions, and droughts. It wasn't until Edmond Halley, studying the paths of earlier comets as past astronomers recorded them, realized that some of the previous comets were actually the same comet returning again and again. Halley used his observations to predict that a comet that appeared in 1682 would return again in 1758. Halley's correct prediction helped demystify comets and show that they are not divine omens at all, but simply celestial objects that are subject to the same laws of physics as the Earth, moon, and planets.

The oldest science of them all has evolved over thousands of years to become the most technologically advanced science, but one thing has remained the same: astronomers continue to use observations of the sky to make predictions about the future. Astronomers have determined that our sun will eventually expand into a red giant before casting off its outer layers and ending its life as a white dwarf. They have predicted that our galaxy will one day collide with our larger neighbor Andromeda. Einstein's theories predicted the existence of black holes, gravitational waves, and wormholes. Black holes were confirmed in 1971 and gravitational waves were measured in 2015, but wormholes remain just a prediction—at least for now. The pace of discovery in astronomy is faster than ever before, and today hardly a week goes by without the announcement of some new discovery in astronomy.

There have been far too many advances in astronomy over the centuries to list them all here. In fact, the advances in astronomy that have been made in the

past 5 years alone are more than enough to fill a book this size. This timeline includes the most important and sometimes most surprising discoveries in astronomy from its earliest days to the present. All of the B.C. dates in this timeline cannot be known for certain and are approximate.

8000 B.C.

The Warren Field calendar in Scotland is built. This is a series of 12 pits dug into the ground that once probably held wooden posts. The pits correlate with phases of the moon, making this the oldest known astronomical calendar. It is believed that prehistoric hunter/gatherers used this calendar to predict the changing of the seasons and the migration times of different animal prey.

4900 B.C.

The Goseck circle is built in Germany. The Goseck circle is a set of large concentric circles made of ditches and mounds in the ground, with two circular wooden fences. The outer fence that enclosed all the other circles had a diameter of 246 feet. The two gates in that fence aligned perfectly with sunrise and sunset on the winter solstice.

3000–1500 B.C.

Stonehenge is a large circle of monoliths in southern England that was built and rebuilt over a period of about 15 centuries. Stonehenge as we know it today was finished around 1500 B.C. It is about 100 feet in diameter and is made up of massive rectangular blocks of stone—the largest is 30 feet tall and weighs 40 tons. The stones are aligned so that small gaps in the stones line up with the direction of sunrise on the summer solstice and sunset on the winter solstice.

2300 B.C.

The Sumerians record the movements of the five planets visible to the naked eye and also name the 12 constellations of the zodiac.

2296 B.C.

The first recorded observation of a comet by astronomers in China.

2137 B.C.

First recorded solar eclipse, also by astronomers in China.

1500 B.C.

The earliest known sundial is developed in Egypt. A sundial is a clock for telling the time of day based on the position of a shadow cast by the sun.

The ancient emperors of China based their calendars on the movements of the sun and moon, and also believed that the stars predicted the future, so they employed a large number of astronomers to keep detailed records of the night skies. As a result, many of the earliest astronomical observations available to us today were made thousands of years ago by Chinese astronomers.

ASTRONOMY TIMELINE

151

ASTRONOMY TIMELINE

1350 B.C.
The Babylonians compile the first star catalog, listing 36 stars.

1300 B.C.
Chinese astronomers begin an ongoing study of eclipses, recording 900 solar eclipses and 600 lunar eclipses over the next 2,600 years.

800 B.C.
Chinese astronomers record what appear to be the first observations of dark spots on the sun known as sunspots. The existence of sunspots would not actually be confirmed for another 2,400 years, after the discovery of the telescope.

The scientist philosopher Anaxagoras was once asked what the purpose is of being born. He answered, "The investigation of the sun, moon, and heaven."

450 B.C.
Greek philosopher Anaxagoras suggests that the sun and stars are fiery pieces of rock, the sun is bigger than the mainland of Greece, and the moon's light is reflected sunlight.
His theory might be based on having seen a meteorite the size of a wagon that supposedly landed in Greece when Anaxagoras was a young man. He was the first person to explain that a lunar eclipse occurs when the moon passes through Earth's shadow.

270 B.C.
In Greece, Aristarchus of Samos claims the sun is the center of the solar system and places the planets in orbits in the correct order around the sun. He also claims that stars are distant suns. His theory seems to have gained some support despite being unprovable at the time, until about 400 years later when Ptolemy rejected it and argued once more for an Earth-centered solar system instead. Ptolemy's views were then widely accepted.

Aristarchus calculated that the sun is almost 10 times larger in diameter than the Earth, and reasoned that since the sun is so much bigger, Earth must orbit the sun rather than the other way around.
The sun's diameter is actually about 109 times larger than Earth's. Aristarchus's calculations would have been right except that the numbers he had to work with were wrong.

240 B.C.
Chinese astronomers record the first known appearance of Halley's Comet.

200 B.C. Greek mathematician Eratosthenes calculates the circumference of the Earth based on the lengths of the noon shadows in two cities in Egypt and is within 15% of the correct value.

Eratosthenes loved all kinds of learning and became good at many things—astronomy, poetry, math, music, and more—but he was never the best at anything. His critics nicknamed him "Beta," after the second letter of the Greek alphabet, saying that Eratosthenes was always second best.

130 B.C. Greek astronomer Hipparchus calculates the distance from the Earth to the moon based on measurements made during a solar eclipse. His calculated distance is within 4% of the actual distance.

87 B.C. The Antikythera mechanism in ancient Greece predicts the positions of the sun, moon, and planets for any given date, along with eclipses. The Antikythera mechanism is a clockwork device made up of about 30 interlocking gears inside a wooden box. It was found corroded and in pieces in a shipwreck in the Aegean Sea in 1900.

140 A.D. Greek mathematician and scientist Ptolemy asserts that the Earth is the center of the universe, and that the sun, moon, planets, and stars all circle the Earth. This was widely accepted and held to be true for almost 1,400 years until Copernicus successfully refuted it.

Although Ptolemy was wrong about the sun orbiting the Earth, his geocentric (Earth-centered) model was able to accurately predict the positions of the stars and planets in the sky on any given date, and this helped convince everyone that he was right.

185 The first supernova ever recorded is seen by Chinese astronomers. They called it a "guest star," which was visible for eight months. In 2006, astronomers discovered the supernova remnant left over from this explosion.

499 In India, astronomer Aryabhata proposes that the Earth spins on its axis and calculates the time it takes the planets to complete one orbit around the sun.

The Ptolemaic system

ASTRONOMY TIMELINE

153

ASTRONOMY TIMELINE

1006
Chinese astronomers record another supernova, now known as SN 1006. This supernova is also recorded by astronomers in the Middle East and Europe.

1054
Chinese astronomers observe supernova SN 1054. The remains of that supernova are known as the Crab Nebula.

1531
Peter Apian, studying what would later become known as Halley's Comet, notes that its tail is always pointed away from the sun, and creates detailed color diagrams of the comet's path through the sky.

1543
Shortly before his death Nicolaus Copernicus publishes his theory in which the sun is the center of the universe and the Earth rotates on an axis while orbiting around the sun along with the other planets and stars. Copernicus had actually developed his heliocentric (sun-centered) theory at least 11 years earlier, but he refused to publish it because it contradicted church teachings and Ptolemy's Earth-centered model of the solar system, and he was afraid of being ridiculed or prosecuted for his views. Most of the astronomers of his time rejected Copernicus's theories, but they were the first big step toward our modern understanding of the universe. Copernicus is now considered the father of modern astronomy.

> Astronomy started out as a hobby for Copernicus. He didn't write his first paper detailing his work in astronomy until he was about 40 years old.

1560
Astronomers predict a total solar eclipse for August 21, and when it happens just as predicted, 14-year-old Tycho Brahe is so amazed he decides to become an astronomer so he can make predictions, too. He begins making detailed observations of the movement of the planets in the sky. Within 3 years, he realizes that his observations are more accurate than the data tables that are being used by astronomers. He continues making careful observations of planetary movement, but he does not share most of his knowledge with other astronomers.

> When Tycho Brahe was 20 years old, he got into a sword fight with another student over which of them was a better mathematician, and part of his nose was cut off in the duel. For the rest of his life Tycho Brahe wore a fake nose tip made out of brass.

| 1572 | A supernova appears in November and is widely recorded. After studying the "new star," Tycho Brahe published a short book called *De nova et nullius aevi memoria prius visa stella* (Latin for "Concerning the Star, New and Never Before Seen in the Life or Memory of Anyone"). Because of his writings about it, this supernova came to be known as Tycho's Supernova. |

| 1576 | Englishman Thomas Digges, who was also studying the supernova of 1572, proposes that there is not a celestial sphere with stars on it encircling the Earth, and instead that the stars are spread out throughout space at various distances from Earth. |

| 1584 | Italian astronomer and mathematician Giordano Bruno suggests that the universe is infinite and has no center, and that stars are other suns that are orbited by planets of their own that might contain alien life. |

Although Giordano Bruno was right about these things, he had no evidence at all to support his claims, and he was really just making things up. Some historians say Bruno was not a good scientist and others say he wasn't even a scientist at all, since science relies on evidence and Bruno didn't seem to care whether he had any evidence or not.

| 1590's | William Gilbert creates a hand-drawn map of the moon. He labels the dark areas as continents and the bright areas as seas, in contrast to other astronomers of his time (including Galileo) who believe the dark areas are seas and the bright areas are continents. |

| 1596 | German pastor and amateur astronomer David Fabricius discovers a new kind of object in the sky—a star whose brightness increases and decreases in a regular pattern over time. This was the first variable star known to astronomers. |

| 1608 | The invention of the telescope by Dutch eyeglass maker Hans Lippershey. The invention was originally called a spyglass and was intended only for viewing distant objects on Earth, until Galileo aimed his at the sky in 1609 and revolutionized the field of astronomy. |

ASTRONOMY TIMELINE

ASTRONOMY TIMELINE

1609

Johannes Kepler publishes his first two laws of planetary motion, in which for the first time planetary orbits are described as elliptical instead of circular. Kepler's third and final law of planetary motion is published 10 years later in 1619. Many astronomers at the time (including Galileo) didn't believe orbits were elliptical, but Kepler's laws are now considered among the basic laws of astronomy.

Tycho Brahe was good at making accurate observations of the motion of the planets, but he didn't know how to turn his observations into mathematical equations. Johannes Kepler was good at developing mathematical equations, but he needed detailed observations to compare his calculations to in order to know if they were correct. When Kepler asked Brahe to share his information about planetary orbits, Brahe invited Kepler to come and work as his assistant—but when he got there, Brahe still wouldn't share his knowledge of the planets' orbits with him. When Brahe died the next year, Kepler finally got his hands on Brahe's notes and was then able to develop his three laws of planetary motion that are still used today.

Johannes Kepler

1610

The first observation of sunspots with a telescope, showing that our sun goes through periods of higher activity and lower activity, and is in fact a variable star whose variability is very low.

Galileo publishes *The Starry Message* (sometimes called *The Starry Messenger*), a booklet containing drawings and descriptions of the moon, stars, and Jupiter's moons based on his observations through a telescope.

Galileo discovers Saturn's rings, but his early telescope isn't strong enough to show them as rings. Instead Saturn looked like a star with two smaller stars right next to it, one on each side.

Galileo discovered Jupiter's four largest moons on January 7, 1610, but Simon Marius claimed that he discovered them first, on December 29, 1609. Marius then named the moons Io, Callisto, Ganymede, and Europa. However, there were two different calendars in use at the time—Galileo was using the Gregorian calendar and Marius was using the Julian calendar. January 7, 1610 on Galileo's Gregorian calendar was December 28, 1609 on Marius's Julian calendar, so it turns out that Galileo discovered the moons one day before Marius did. Even so, the names Marius gave the moons are the ones we still use today.

1655 Christiaan Huygens realizes that the bright spots Galileo saw surrounding Saturn are really a flat disk, which he believes to be solid. Huygens also discovers Saturn's largest moon Titan the same year.

1668 Isaac Newton builds the first working reflecting telescope, which bounces light off curved mirrors instead of passing light through curved glass lenses. Most large optical telescopes today, including the Hubble Space Telescope, are reflecting telescopes.

1671 Isaac Newton discovers that by passing light through prisms, light can be separated into different colors and reassembled back into white light. He theorizes that light is made up of different-colored particles that he called *corpuscles*, moving at different speeds.

1687 Isaac Newton publishes his laws of motion and universal gravitation, which say that the same force of gravity that we feel in everyday life is also what controls the motions of the celestial bodies.

1705 Edmond Halley discovers that many of the reported comet sightings over previous centuries were in fact the same comet returning about every 76 years, and correctly predicts that it will return again in 1758.

1750 Thomas Wright says that the Milky Way appears in the sky as a white smear because our sun is located in a flat layer of stars. He also proposes that are other galaxies outside of our own.

1771 Charles Messier compiles his first catalog of objects in deep space, listing 45 nebulas, star clusters, and galaxies.

Messier was a comet hunter who was frustrated by objects in deep space that resembled the fuzzy light from a comet and kept distracting him in his searches, so he made a list of those objects so that he would stop getting confused by them. An expanded version of his catalog of deep space objects is still used by astronomers today.

1781 William Hershel discovers Uranus. This is the first new planet to be discovered since ancient times, and makes the amateur astronomer an instant celebrity.

ASTRONOMY TIMELINE

ASTRONOMY TIMELINE

1783

John Michell proposes that if a star is massive enough, its own gravity would pull in whatever light it emits. He calls these hypothetical objects *dark stars*, but they are similar in many ways to what we call *black holes*.

Caroline Hershel discovers three new nebulas. Over her career she will also discover eight comets and with her brother William, create a listing of objects in deep space that will eventually form the basis for the New General Catalogue.

William Hershel was a professional musician and conductor who dabbled in astronomy in his spare time. His younger sister Caroline was a professional singer who performed at some of his concerts and also studied astronomy on the side. After William Hershel discovered Uranus in 1781, both he and Caroline became full-time astronomers.

1801

Giuseppe Piazzi discovers Ceres, the largest asteroid in the asteroid belt. Ceres was originally considered a planet, but was reclassified as an asteroid in the 1850s when many more objects in similar orbits were discovered. Ceres was reclassified again in 2006, this time as a dwarf planet.

1814

Joseph von Fraunhofer discovers dark lines in the sun's emission spectrum. Scientists will later determine that the dark lines are due to sunlight being absorbed by certain atoms, and this information will eventually be used to learn about the chemical composition of clouds of gas in outer space.

1838

The first reliable distance to another star is calculated. Friedrich Bessel determines the distance to a binary star in the constellation Cygnus to be 10.4 light-years. Further measurements and calculations over the next 30 years refined this distance to 11.36 light-years, close to the accepted distance today of 11.41 light-years.

1840

The very first photographs were called *daguerreotypes*, and were black and white images made on metal plates. In 1840, the first daguerreotype was made of the moon, marking the beginning of astrophotography.

One of the first pictures ever taken of the moon by Dr. J. W. Draper of New York, 1840.

1846 — Urbain Le Verrier mathematically predicts the position of an unknown planet outside of the orbit of Uranus, and Neptune is discovered almost exactly where Le Verrier says it should be.

Le Verrier wanted to name the newly discovered planet "Le Verrier" after himself, but other scientists chose Neptune instead. All of the planets except Earth are named after mythological deities.

1850 — The first photograph of a star other than the sun. (Vega, the brightest star in the constellation Lyra.)

1862 — Husband and wife William and Margaret Huggins carefully study the wavelengths of light coming from objects in space and determine that stars are made out of the same materials as the sun, proving for the first time that the sun is a star and that stars are distant suns.

1877 — Giovanni Schiaparelli describes the existence of what looks like channels in the surface of Mars. The Italian word *canali* is incorrectly translated to English as "canals," leading some people to believe that they are the remains of an ancient Martian civilization. Studies of Mars in the 20th century reveal that Schiaparelli's *canali* were actually an optical illusion and there never were any channels.

Asaph Hall discovers two moons orbiting Mars and names them Phobos (Fear) and Deimos (Terror) after the two sons of Ares in Greek mythology.

Astronomer Percival Lowell believed the canals on Mars were real. He spent 15 years at his Lowell Observatory in Arizona observing and mapping what he thought was an extensive canal system, and between 1895 and 1908 he wrote three books about life on Mars. Although the scientific community disagreed with Lowell's conclusions, his books inspired many writers of that era including H.G. Wells (*The War of the Worlds*) and Edgar Rice Burroughs (*A Princess of Mars*), and helped establish the genre of outer space alien science fiction.

1888 — The first edition of the New General Catalogue (NGC) is published. The NGC is the most comprehensive listing of all deep space objects ever discovered, and now includes more than 13,000 objects such as galaxies, nebulas, and star clusters.

ASTRONOMY TIMELINE

ASTRONOMY TIMELINE

1904
Johannes Hartmann discovers the existence of interstellar matter based on light from distant stars that never reaches Earth.

Jacobus Kapteyn discovers the first evidence that the Milky Way galaxy is rotating. This is confirmed 23 years later by Jan Oort.

1907
Hermann Minkowski, who was one of Albert Einstein's college math professors, invents spacetime by treating time and three-dimensional space as one combined object in his mathematical equations.

1911
The first H-R diagram is published, comparing the brightness of stars with their temperatures. This will ultimately lead to an understanding of how stars grow and change over their lifetimes.

1912
Henrietta Swan Leavitt shows how Cepheid variable stars can be used to measure the distance to far-off objects in space, making it possible for the first time to determine how far away other galaxies are.

Henrietta Swan Leavitt

1915
Albert Einstein publishes his general theory of relativity, which describes gravity as the result of masses curving the spacetime around them. His theory also predicts the existence of black holes (discovered in 1971) and gravitational waves (detected in 2015).

Imagination is more important than knowledge.
—Albert Einstein

Robert Innes discovers Proxima Centauri, the nearest star to our sun. Proxima Centauri is a red dwarf that is too dim to see with the naked eye.

1918
Harlow Shapley determines the size and shape of the Milky Way, along with the sun's position in it.

Harlow Shapley was a newspaper reporter who went to college to study journalism, but the university was not offering journalism classes for another year. Shapely said he decided instead to study the first thing in the course listings, but when he couldn't pronounce "archaeology," he went on to the next subject, astronomy, and studied that.

1920

Arthur Eddington proposes that the sun's energy comes from fusion.

Meghnad Saha discovers how to determine a star's temperature and chemical composition from the spectrum of light it gives off.

1924

Using Henrietta Swan Leavitt's method for measuring distances in space, Edwin Hubble discovers that Andromeda is not a nebula within the Milky Way as had previously been believed, but is actually another galaxy outside of our own. This is the first discovery of another galaxy.

1925

Cecilia Payne shows that all stars, no matter what type, are made up almost entirely of hydrogen and helium. Until this time it was assumed that the sun and planets were made of more or less the same stuff, and that different types of stars were made of different materials.

1927

Jan Oort discovers that the center of the Milky Way galaxy is in the direction of the constellation Sagittarius.

Georges Lemaître proposes that the universe is expanding in every direction from its original size. This contradicts the widely held belief that the universe has a fixed size, and even Albert Einstein rejects Lemaître's idea. (Edwin Hubble is often credited with the discovery of an expanding universe because Lemaître published his work in a Belgian scientific journal whereas Hubble's discovery 2 years later was published in English and was more widely read.)

In 1931, Georges Lemaître modified his 1927 theory to state that the universe began from a "cosmic egg" which exploded to form the universe. Astronomer Fred Hoyle rejected the idea and in 1949 referred to it dismissively as "the Big Bang theory."

1930

After nearly a year of searching for a suspected ninth planet, Clyde Tombaugh discovers Pluto. Later it is found that Pluto had been observed at least 16 times between 1906 and 1915, but nobody at the time realized what it was.

Nineteen-year-old Subrahmanyan Chandrasekhar calculates the maximum mass a white dwarf can have, which is equal to 1.4 solar masses. Any star whose core has a greater mass than that will become a neutron star or a black hole when it dies. This cutoff is known as the Chandrasekhar limit.

ASTRONOMY TIMELINE

ASTRONOMY TIMELINE

1932
The first radio telescope is built. This allows astronomers to detect objects in space such as pulsars and quasars that do not give off visible light.

1933
Fritz Zwicky and Walter Baade coin the term *supernova* for an exploding star. They also propose the existence of neutron stars and correctly hypothesize that supernovas occur when normal stars turn into neutron stars. This same year Zwicky also provides evidence that most of the mass of the universe is made up of undetectable dark matter.

1950
Jan Oort predicts the existence of the Oort cloud surrounding our solar system.

1951
Gerard Kuiper proposes the existence of a belt of small objects lying outside the orbit of Neptune. He believes such a belt might have formed at one point in our solar system's past, but thought that gravity would have broken it up by now and little or nothing would remain. When the Kuiper belt is discovered in the early 1990s, it is named after him.

1957
The Soviet Union launches the first artificial satellite, Sputnik 1, into orbit.

1958
In response to the launch of Sputnik 1, the United States forms NASA, the National Aeronautics and Space Agency.

1959
The Soviet probe Luna 3 takes the first ever photos of the far side of the moon, showing a side of the moon humans have never seen before. It is far rougher and more cratered than the side that faces Earth.

1961
Russian cosmonaut Yuri Gagarin becomes the first man in space.

This poster from the early 1960s celebrates the success of the Russian space program, saying "Glory to the Russian people, the pioneers of space!"

1962
Space probe Mariner 2 flies past Venus, becoming the first probe to visit another planet.

1963
Maarten Schmidt discovers the first visible quasar. He knows it is not a star but doesn't know what it is, so he calls it a "quasi-stellar radio source."

In 1964, astrophysicist Hong-Yee Chiu wrote a paper about Maarten Schmidt's newly-discovered radio source, but Chiu didn't feel like writing out "quasi-stellar radio source" every time he mentioned it, so he shortened it to "quasar" (p. 43). Today we know quasars are not "quasi-stellar" at all, but we still use Chiu's shortened version of the name.

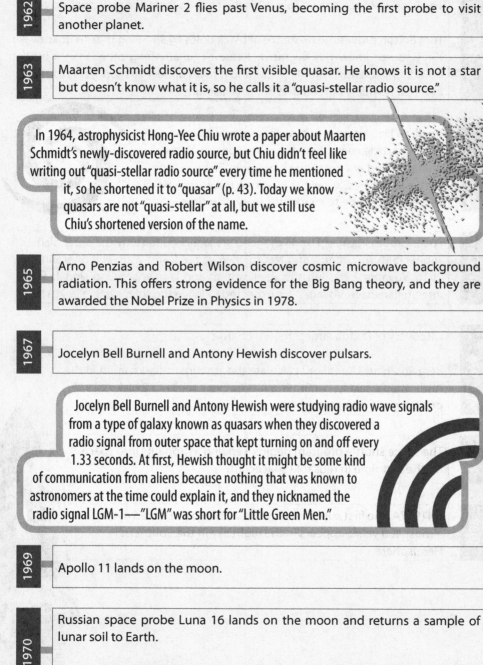

1965
Arno Penzias and Robert Wilson discover cosmic microwave background radiation. This offers strong evidence for the Big Bang theory, and they are awarded the Nobel Prize in Physics in 1978.

1967
Jocelyn Bell Burnell and Antony Hewish discover pulsars.

Jocelyn Bell Burnell and Antony Hewish were studying radio wave signals from a type of galaxy known as quasars when they discovered a radio signal from outer space that kept turning on and off every 1.33 seconds. At first, Hewish thought it might be some kind of communication from aliens because nothing that was known to astronomers at the time could explain it, and they nicknamed the radio signal LGM-1—"LGM" was short for "Little Green Men."

1969
Apollo 11 lands on the moon.

1970
Russian space probe Luna 16 lands on the moon and returns a sample of lunar soil to Earth.

Russian space probe Venera 7 lands on Venus, becoming the first successful landing on another planet.

ASTRONOMY TIMELINE

163

ASTRONOMY TIMELINE

1971

The Russian space station Salyut 1 is the first space station ever put into orbit.

Tom Bolton proves the existence of black holes by showing that an unknown X-ray source known as Cygnus X-1 cannot be anything other than a black hole. Many scientists are skeptical, and it takes almost 20 more years of study before it is widely agreed that Bolton was right.

1974

Stephen Hawking proposes that black holes can create particles near their event horizons, at a cost of matter and energy to the black hole. The emission of these particles, known as Hawking radiation, can cause a black hole to evaporate away over time.

1977

Space probes Voyager 1 and Voyager 2 are launched to study the outer planets, Jupiter, Saturn, Uranus, and Neptune. Voyager 1 and 2 are still operating in 2016. Voyager 1 has left the solar system and is now sending signals from interstellar space. Voyager 2 is expected to leave the solar system in 2016.

1978

Discovery of Pluto's largest moon, Charon.

Vera Rubin and Kent Ford calculate the amount of dark matter in the Andromeda galaxy, confirming for the first time Fritz Zwicky's 1933 prediction of dark matter.

1981

The space shuttle program begins, sending astronauts into space for the first time in reusable spacecraft.

1987

SN1987A, the first supernova that is visible to the naked eye in almost 400 years, appears in the night sky in the Southern Hemisphere.

1990 The Hubble Space Telescope is put into orbit, but a problem with one of the mirrors results in fuzzy, out-of-focus images. The problem is fixed by Space Shuttle astronauts in 1993.

1992 The first confirmation of the existence of exoplanets.

The first Mars rover was named after a former slave named Isabella Baumfree who changed her name to Sojourner Truth and made it her life's work to "travel up and down the land," working to end slavery and fight for more rights for women. Her chosen name Sojourner means "traveler."

1997 The Mars Pathfinder rover, named Sojourner, lands on Mars and begins collecting data.

1998 The International Space Station is sent into orbit.

1999 The Chandra X-Ray Observatory telescope is launched into Earth's orbit and begins receiving X-rays from deep space. The data is transmitted to Earth where it is converted into images of such things as galaxies and nebulas.

2001 Near Earth Asteroid Rendezvous—Shoemaker (NEAR-Shoemaker) becomes the first probe to land on an asteroid.

2004 Twin Mars rovers Spirit and Opportunity land and begin collecting data.

The Cassini–Huygens space probe reaches Saturn. Orbiter Cassini sends back data about Saturn and its rings.

A color-enhanced photo of two of Saturn's major rings taken by Cassini shows dusty particles in Saturn's C ring toward the left (in red) giving way to cleaner icy particles in Saturn's B ring on the right (in blue). Saturn itself would be off to the left of this photo.

ASTRONOMY TIMELINE

165

2005

The Huygens lander from the Cassini–Huygens space probe lands on Saturn's moon Titan, becoming the first successful landing on an alien moon.

2006

Pluto is reclassified as a dwarf planet following the discovery of Eris in 2005.

Space probe Stardust, launched in 1999, successfully returns to Earth a capsule of dust and particles collected from the coma of Comet Wild 2.

Brian May, the guitar player for the rock band **Queen**, was a graduate student in astrophysics studying the motion of dust clouds in the solar system when his band suddenly became popular. He quit graduate school in 1974 and became an international rock star. In 2006, he returned to graduate school to finish his research, and completed his Ph.D. at Imperial College London in 2007. He was able to pick up where he left off because between 1974 and 2006 almost no other research was done in the subject he was studying.

2009

The Kepler space observatory is launched, designed specifically to search for exoplanets.

2011

MESSENGER becomes the first space probe to orbit the planet Mercury.

Dawn becomes the first space probe to orbit an asteroid, Vesta.

2012

Curiosity, the largest and most technologically advanced Mars rover, lands on Mars. Its mission includes looking for signs of life.

The Voyager 1 space probe, launched in 1977, leaves the solar system and transmits data from interstellar space.

2014 The European Space Agency's Rosetta space probe orbits a comet named 67P/Churyumov–Gerasimenko and sends back photos of the surface that show cliffs almost 500 feet high and boulders the size of houses. Rosetta sends down a lander called Philae, which successfully lands on the comet.

These images of comet 67P/Churyumov–Gerasimenko were taken by Rosetta between August and November 2014.

2015 The space probe New Horizons flies past Pluto, providing the first close-up images of Pluto.

The Mars Reconnaissance Orbiter provides evidence that liquid water flows intermittently on the surface of Mars.

Gravitational waves are first detected, resulting from a collision between two black holes 1.3 billion light-years away.

View of Pluto on July 14, 2015.

ADDITIONAL READINGS

FOR YOUNGER READERS

The Best Book of Spaceships by Ian Graham (Kingfisher, 1998)—Includes an overview of the solar system followed by an introduction to rockets and how they work. Also covers moon missions, the space shuttle, working in space, the Hubble telescope, and space probes. 32 pages.

I Wonder Why Stars Twinkle by Carole Stott (Kingfisher, 2011)—Thirty questions you might ask about space, such as "Will the sun ever go out?" and "How fast can rockets go?", as well as "Which planet's moons look like potatoes?", "Which planet is tipped over?", and "Which is the red planet?" 32 pages.

A Journey Through Space by Steve Parker (QEB Publishing, 2015)—Cartoon drawings of a boy in a space ship traveling through the solar system, with a few sentences about each planet, the moon, and the asteroid belt, along the way. Also touches on constellations, the Milky Way, black holes, neutron stars, and the big bang theory. 48 pages.

National Geographic Kids First Big Book of Space by Catherine D. Hughes (2012)—This book uses a large font and provides basic facts, mostly about the solar system. 128 pages.

Night Wonders by Jane Anne Peddicord (Charlesbridge, 2005)—This rhyming picture book about riding a beam of light through our solar system into intergalactic space and back offers a different approach to science. Each page has a short poem about a particular aspect of astronomy, along with a few sentences explaining the science behind the rhyme. 32 pages.

Our Solar System and Beyond by Flying Frog Publishing (2014)—A board book that covers the solar system and its formation. Also includes stars, stargazing, and space exploration. Available only from Barnes & Noble. 48 pages.

Read, Search, & Find: Space by Kidsbooks (2013)—Each two-page spread has one large picture with a sidebar containing six to eight smaller images from that picture with one or two sentences explaining each one. The first half of the book includes an introduction to astronomy and some pages on the solar system, and the last half of the book is about space exploration. 32 pages.

FOR SPACE ENTHUSIASTS IN GRADES 3-6

Adventures in the Real World: The Story of the Exploration of Space by Penny Clarke (Sterling, 2013)—Discover the evolution of space exploration from the earliest rockets in 1926 to space probes and the ISS, to future Mars colonies. Learn about the people, process, and technology of space exploration. 64 pages.

Child's Introduction to the Night Sky: The Story of the Stars, Planets, and Constellations—and How You Can find Them in the Night Sky by Michael Driscoll (Black Dog & Leventhal, 2004)—Includes an overview and history of astronomy, the solar system, and sections on the jobs of astronomers and astronauts. The last third of the book is devoted to constellations. 96 pages.

Discovery Spaceopedia: The Complete Guide to Everything Space by Discovery (Liberty Street, 2015)—About half of this book is devoted to the solar system, about a quarter to stars and galaxies, and the rest to cosmology and space exploration. 192 pages.

DK Eyewitness Books: Universe by DK Publishing (2015)—After a brief section on cosmology, the book focuses on the solar system, then goes into a shorter section about deep space and stars. 72 pages.

Eye Wonder: Space by Carole Stott (DK Publishing, 2016)—Includes short paragraphs and many photos and illustrations on each two-page spread. About half the book is devoted to the solar system, a quarter to deep space, and a quarter to space exploration. There are eight pages of quizzes and games at the end of the book. 64 pages.

Inside Stars by Andra Serlin Abramson (Sterling, 2011)—After a section on cosmology, this book focuses on stars—their formation, classification of stars, processes that occur within stars, multiple star systems, and stellar evolution and death. 48 pages.

ADDITIONAL READINGS

My Tourist Guide to the Solar System ... and Beyond by DK Publishing (2012)—Written as a travel guide to various places in the solar system, this book points out the unique and interesting aspects of each place, such as geysers, mountains, underground oceans, and other sightseeing opportunities a traveler from Earth might enjoy. It even includes reviews from previous travelers who have been to each location, and they are not always positive. 64 pages.

Night Sky Atlas by DK Publishing (2007)— The focus of this book is on identifying and finding constellations. It breaks up the night sky into sections and goes month by month through the year showing which constellations are visible in the Northern and Southern Hemispheres. There is detailed information about each constellation, along with a section on stellar evolution and brief biographies of various astronomers throughout history. Includes acetate overlays and a CD ROM. 48 pages.

ScienceSaurus: A Student Handbook, Grades 6–8 by Great Source Education Group (2005)—This 544-page kid-friendly science book has only 17 pages devoted to astronomy, but it covers a number of difficult topics and does it well. Some of the topics covered include phases of the moon, tides, eclipses, objects in the solar system, H-R diagrams, apparent and absolute magnitude, and galaxy types. 544 pages.

Seeing Stars: The McDonald Observatory—Its Science & Astronomers by Mark Mitchell (Eakin, 1997)—A history of the McDonald Observatory in Texas and some of the astronomers who worked there, with astronomy facts woven into the narrative. The behind-the-scenes information about the construction of the observatory and what it's like to be an astronomer working at an observatory is hard to find in newer books. 100 pages.

Space Encyclopedia: A Tour of Our Solar System and Beyond by David A. Aguilar (National Geographic, 2013)—A comprehensive book about space intended for grades 5 and up, covering cosmology, the solar system, deep space astronomy, exoplanets, and the future of space exploration. Past and present space exploration is woven throughout the book. 192 pages.

FOR ADVANCED READERS (AND THEIR PARENTS)

The 50 Most Extreme Places in Our Solar System by David Baker and Todd Ratcliff (Bleknap, Press 2010)—Describes some of the most interesting and bizarre places in our solar system, from icy volcanoes to a moon that smells like a giant rotten egg. The material is presented in 50 short chapters, each about six pages long, with color photos and illustrations. 304 pages.

Eyewitness Explorer: Night Sky Detective by Ben Morgan (DK Publishing, 2015)—Two-page spreads about the solar system. Most spreads also include science activities such as how to keep track of lunar phases for a month, how to recreate the red soil of Mars, and how to "see" and track the movement of sunspots without looking at the sun. 72 pages.

Gastrophysics by Stephen Hughes (available only on iTunes, 2015)—This eBook describes concepts in astrophysics, such as how the mass of an object warps spacetime around it, through analogies and activities involving food and kitchen appliances. It includes activities that can be done in the kitchen at home. 417 pages.

The Planets by DK Publishing (2014)—Like its companion volume *Space!*, this is a single-volume encyclopedia with high-quality images that goes into much greater detail in every subject, but still presents the information in two-page spreads. 256 pages.

Rocket Science for the Rest of Us by Ben Gilliland (DK Publishing, 2015)—This is not just about rockets and space exploration, but covers a broad range of topics in astronomy and physics. The author explains a lot of the underlying physics behind the workings of the universe, including such things as quarks and string theory. 192 pages.

Space! by DK Publishing (2015)—This book and its companion book *The Planets* are single-volume visual encyclopedias. They have much more information and go into a deeper level of detail than a usual DK science book, but still present the information in two-page spreads. 208 pages.

ADDITIONAL READINGS

ONLINE RESOURCES

Space Facts (http://space-facts.com)—A fantastic kid-friendly site, easy to navigate, with lots of facts and photos. The site includes information about the solar system and galaxies.

Space.com (http://www.space.com)—With some material for kids and some for adults, space.com covers just about everything you would ever want to know about astronomy and keeps up with the fast pace of new discoveries.

Science News (https://www.sciencenews.org)—Science News is one of the best resources for learning about new scientific discoveries. It takes technical publications from all areas of science and describe them in terms a non-scientist can understand.

Everyday Cosmology (http://cosmology.carnegiescience.edu)—An astronomy timeline from 1610 to 2000 that contains detailed accounts of selected events. Some of the timeline entries also include activities that tie in to the particular event of that timeline entry.

ABOUT THE AUTHORS

Amy Anderson graduated summa cum laude from Austin College in 2015 with a triple major in physics, theater, and math, and a minor in classical civilization. She is currently a graduate student in astrophysics at Rice University. Amy shares her middle name with one of Neptune's moons.

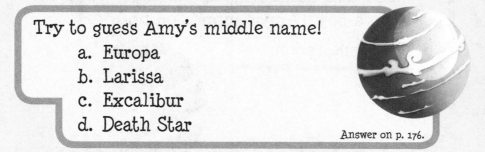

Try to guess Amy's middle name!
- a. Europa
- b. Larissa
- c. Excalibur
- d. Death Star

Answer on p. 176.

Brian Anderson is Amy's dad. He has a master's degree in marine science and a Ph.D. in chemistry, both from the University of Texas, as well as a bachelor's degree in chemistry from Knox College. His past jobs include university lecturer, hazardous waste operations, and backstage security at rock concerts. Brian is the author of the Zack Proton outer space comedy chapter books and wrote the teen horror film *Raven Road*. In the summertime, Brian makes custom piñatas at http://www.pinataboy.com.

Amy's middle name is . . .

a. Europa is one of Jupiter's moons.

b. Correct! Larissa is one of Neptune's tiny moons, named after a water nymph from Greek mythology.

c. Excalibur is the name of King Arthur's sword, and is what Brian wanted to name Amy if she had been a boy. (Amy's mom said no.)

d. That's no moon.

ABOUT THE AUTHORS

INDEX

INDEX

INDEX

INDEX

INDEX

IMAGE CREDITS

The publisher would like to thank the following for their permission to reproduce their illustrations:

Abbreviation key: t–top; m–middle; b–bottom

5: NASA/WMAP Science Team; 6: NASA/ESA/D. Harvey (École Polytechnique Fédérale de Lausanne, Switzerland)/R. Massey (Durham University, UK)/HST Frontier Fields; 20: Michael Owen/John Blondin–North Carolina State University; 21: X-ray–NASA/CXC/CfA/R.Kraft et al.; Submillimeter–MPIfR/ESO/APEX/A.Weiss et al.; Optical–ESO/WFI (t), WikiCommons/Skatebiker (b); 22: Pixabay/skeeze; 25: NASA/JPL-Caltech; 28: Dark Horse Observatory; 29: NASA/JPL-Caltech; 31: ESO; 34: ESO; 35: NASA/CXC/SAO; 36: NASA; 37: NASA/CXC/SAO; 38: NASA/ESA/Hubble SM4 ERO Team; 39: NASA/ESA/Z. Levay/R. van der Marel/STScI/T. Hallas/A. Mellinger; 40: Nature Video; 41: ESO/S. Brunier (t), NASA/CXC/JPL-Caltech/STScI (m), ESA/NASA/Hubble (b); 42: ESA/ATG Medialab (t), WikiCommons (b); 43: Nick Risinger; 44: NASA/ESA/STScI/J. Hester/P. Scowen–Arizona State University (t), Ken Crawford (b); 45: X-ray–NASA/CXC/RIKEN/D.Takei et al; Optical–NASA/STScI; Radio–NRAO/VLA; 46: NASA/ESA/C.R. O'Dell–Vanderbilt University; 47: NASA/Penn State University; 48: deviantart/tadp0l3; 49: NASA/ESA/S. Baum and C. O'Dea–RIT/R. Perley and W. Cotton–NRAO/AUI/NSF/Hubble Heritage Team–STScI/AURA; 50: NASA; 51: ESO/C. Snodgrass; 52: NASA/JPL-Caltech (t), NASA/ESA/S. Beckwith–STScI/Hubble Heritage Team STScI/AURA (b); 53: NASA/Hubble Heritage Team/STScI/AURA (t/l), ESO/G. Beccari (t/r), ESA/Hubble/NASA, Acknowledgement: M. Novak (b); 54: NASA (t); 55: NASA/ESA/J. Hester/A. Loll–ASU; 56: NASA; 57: H. Bond–STScI/R. Ciardullo–PSU/WFPC2/HST/NASA; Processing: Forrest Hamilton; 62: NASA/JPL-Caltech/UCLA/MPS/DLR/IDA; 66: X-ray–NASA/CXC/UCL/W. Dunn et al.; Optical–NASA/STScI; 67: NASA/Goddard Space Flight Center Conceptual Image Lab; 69: NASA/JHUAPL/SwRI; 72: NASA/SDO (t), Shane Torgerson (m), NASA/JPL-Caltech/Space Science Institute (b); 74: ESO/L. Calçada/Nick Risinger (t), NASA (b); 76: WikiCommons/Brocken Inaglory; 78: NASA/ESA; 79: NASA/JPL/Space Science Institute; 80: NASA; 81: NASA/JPL-Caltech; 83: NASA/JPL (t), Jeff Dai (m), NASA/JPL (b); 84: NASA/JPL-Caltech/LANL/CNES/IRAP/LPGNantes/CNRS/IAS/MSSS (t), Wikimedia Commons (b); 86: NASA; 87: E. Kolmhofer/H. Raab/Johannes Kepler Observatory; 88: NASA/Steele Hill; 91: NASA/JPL/Space Science Institute; 92: NASA/Goddard; 94: ESA/Hubble/NASA, Acknowledgement: Judy Schmidt (t/r), ESO/L. Calçada (b); 101: NASA/SDO (t), NASA (b); 102: Tunc Tezel; 104: NASA; 106: NASA/Goddard; 107: David Chenette/Joseph B. Gurman/Loren W. Acton (t), NASA/Stephan Heinsius (b); 108: SOHO/EIT Consortium/MDI Team; 109: Sebastian Saarloos (b); 110: WikiCommons/Captmondo; 111: SDO/HMI; 113: NASA/JPL (t), NASA (b); 114: NASA; 115: NASA/ESA/L. Lamy–Observatory of Paris/CNRS/CNES (t), WikiCommons/Booyabazooka (b); 116: SSV/MIPL/Magellan Team/NASA; 117: Matipon Tangmatitham; 120: WikiCommons/Incnis Mrsi; 122: NASA/JPL/DLR (t), Jim Peaco, National Park Service (b); 123: ESO (t), NASA/Ames/JPL-Caltech (b); 126: NASA/JPL/University of Arizona/University of Idaho; 129: NASA (t), NASA/ESA/J. Maíz Apellániz–Instituto de Astrofísica de Andalucía; Spain (m), NASA (b); 130: NASA; 131: NASA (t), Canadian Space Agency (b); 133: WikiCommons (t), NASA (b); 134: NASA (t), Richard Kruse (b); 135: NASA (t), NASA (b); 136: NASA (t/b); 137: NASA (t), Gribben/Saina/Legacy/Web (m), NASA (b); 138: Joost Schuur (t), NASA/JPL/Cornell University/Maas Digital LLC (m), NASA (b); 139: NASA (t), NASA/JPL-Caltech (b); 140: WikiCommons (t), NASA (m), NASA (b); 141: NASA; 142: NASA (t/b); 143: NASA (t/b); 144: NASA; 145: NASA (t/m/b); 147: NASA; 148: Virgin Galactic; 158: J. W. Draper; 160: WikiCommons (t/b); 162: WikiCommons; 164: NASA; 165: NASA/JPL/University of Colorado; 167: ESA/Rosetta/NavCam (t); NASA/JHUAPL/SwRI (b).